Contents

1 The power of Pythagoras

1.1 Pythagoras and right-angled triangles

The great mathematician Pythagoras is best remembered for discovering a relationship (now known as Pythagoras' theorem, although it was certainly not his only theorem) connecting the lengths of the sides of right-angled triangles.

> Pythagoras' theorem states that, in a right-angled triangle with sides a, b and h as shown,
>
> $$h^2 = a^2 + b^2$$
>
>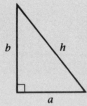

The following tasksheet considers the usefulness of this simple relationship and the influence of Pythagoras on early mathematical thought.

TASKSHEET 1 — Pythagoras' theorem (page 22)

In tasksheet 1 you extended Pythagoras' theorem to three dimensions.

> If d is the long diagonal of a cuboid of dimensions a, b and c, then
>
> $$d^2 = a^2 + b^2 + c^2$$
>
>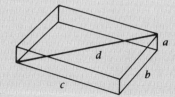

Mathematical methods

The School Mathematics Project

CAMBRIDGE
UNIVERSITY PRESS

Main authors   Simon Baxter
Stan Dolan
Doug French
Andy Hall
Barrie Hunt
Lorna Lyons
Paul Roder
Jeff Searle
David Tall
Thelma Wilson

Project director   Stan Dolan

The authors would like to give special thanks to Ann White for her help in producing the trial edition and in preparing this book for publication.

PUBLISHED BY THE PRESS SYNDICATE OF THE UNIVERSITY OF CAMBRIDGE
The Pitt Building, Trumpington Street, Cambridge CB2 1RP, United Kingdom

CAMBRIDGE UNIVERSITY PRESS
The Edinburgh Building, Cambridge CB2 2RU, United Kingdom
40 West 20th Street, New York, NY 10011–4211, USA
10 Stamford Road, Oakleigh, Melbourne 3166, Australia

First published 1992
Third printing 1998

Produced by Gecko Limited, Bicester, Oxon

Cover design by Iguana Creative Design

Printed in the United Kingdom at the University Press, Cambridge

A catalogue record for this book is available from the British Library

ISBN 0 521 40894 6 paperback

The following trigonometric ratios are sometimes useful.

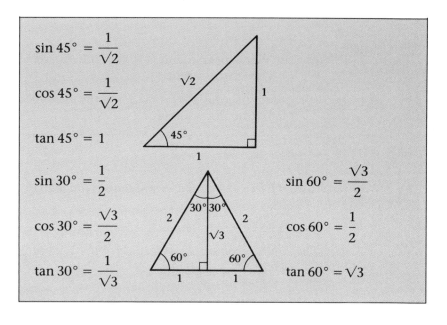

$$\sin 45° = \frac{1}{\sqrt{2}}$$

$$\cos 45° = \frac{1}{\sqrt{2}}$$

$$\tan 45° = 1$$

$$\sin 30° = \frac{1}{2}$$

$$\cos 30° = \frac{\sqrt{3}}{2}$$

$$\tan 30° = \frac{1}{\sqrt{3}}$$

$$\sin 60° = \frac{\sqrt{3}}{2}$$

$$\cos 60° = \frac{1}{2}$$

$$\tan 60° = \sqrt{3}$$

EXERCISE 1

1 Use Pythagoras' theorem for right-angled triangles to find the hypotenuse of

(a)   (b)

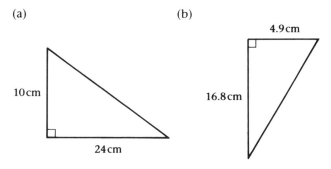

2 Two pigeons fly off Nelson's Column. The first flies 3.7 km due east and lands on the Tower of London. The other flies 0.9 km due south and lands on Westminster Abbey. How far apart are Westminster Abbey and the Tower of London?

3 A ramp is to be built to allow wheelchairs and pushchairs to enter a hotel more easily. The height of the step is 10 cm. The planks to be used are 0.7 m long. How much space will be needed in front of the step?

1.2 The equation of a circle

(a) Use Pythagoras' theorem to find the distance of the point (3, 3) from the origin.

(b) Use Pythagoras' theorem to find the distance of the point (4, 6) from the point (1, 2).

T A S K S H E E T   2   –   Circles and spheres (page 25)

The equation of a circle of radius r about the point (a, b) is

$$(x - a)^2 + (y - b)^2 = r^2$$

When the circle has its centre at the origin, $a = b = 0$, so the equation becomes

$$x^2 + y^2 = r^2$$

This can be rewritten as

$$y = \pm \sqrt{(r^2 - x^2)}$$

E X A M P L E   1

Find the equation of the circle radius 4, centre (2, 3). Does the point (5, 5) lie inside or outside the circle?

S O L U T I O N

The equation of the circle is
$(x - 2)^2 + (y - 3)^2 = 16$.

The distance between the points (2, 3) and (5, 5) is $\sqrt{(3^2 + 2^2)} = \sqrt{13}$.

Since $\sqrt{13}$ is less than the radius of the circle, (5, 5) must lie inside the circle.

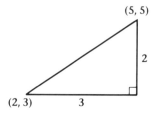

EXERCISE 2

1 Find the equations of the following circles with centre the origin:

(a) radius 15 units   (b) diameter 8 units

(c) circumference 10 units   (d) passing through the point (12, 16)

2 Find the equations of the following circles:

(a) radius 3 units, centre (1, 1)

(b) diameter 16 units, centre $(-4, 6)$

3 A lighthouse has a grid reference (20, 85) on a map, where each unit represents one nautical mile. The light is powerful enough to be seen from up to 18 nautical miles away. Write an equation involving E, the easterly map reference, and N, the northerly map reference, to show the boundary beyond which ships cannot see the lighthouse.

How might this equation be misleading?

4 Find the equation of the sphere, centre (2, 3, 1), radius 4 units.

5 Do the following points lie inside or outside the figures given by the equations?

(a) (3, 2); $(x - 1)^2 + (y - 4)^2 = 9$

(b) $(4, -1)$; $(x + 1)^2 + (y - 2)^2 = 30$

(c) $(-1, 3, 5)$; $(x - 1)^2 + (y + 1)^2 + (z - 3)^2 = 24$

(d) $(-1, 3, 5)$; $(x - 1)^2 + (y + 1)^2 + (z - 3)^2 = 25$

6E Two aerial fireworks are timed to go off at the same time. Relative to an observer on the ground, their centres are at (120, 150, 30) and (160, 180, 40). The radius of the first firework extends to 20 units, that of the second to 30 units. Assuming that both fireworks make a spherical pattern in the sky, will the patterns intersect?

7E Find the centre, radius and equation of the circle passing through the points (6, 9), (13, −8) and (−4, −15).
[Hint: Let the equation be $(x - a)^2 + (y - b)^2 = r^2$.]

8E Find the possible equations of circles, radius 10 units, which pass through the points (10, 9) and (8, −5). Which of these equations describes a circle which also passes through the point (−6, −3)?

1.3 Trigonometric identities

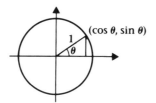

Points on a circle of unit radius, centre the origin, have coordinates given by $(\cos \theta, \sin \theta)$ where θ is the angle measured anticlockwise from the x-axis.

(a) How does the diagram above show that $\sin^2 \theta + \cos^2 \theta = 1$?

(b) Does this result hold for **any** value of θ?

(c) Explain why $\tan \theta = \dfrac{\sin \theta}{\cos \theta}$.

(d) If $\sin \theta = \frac{1}{3}$, what is the value of   (i) $\cos \theta$ (ii) $\tan \theta$?

$$\tan \theta = \frac{\sin \theta}{\cos \theta}; \qquad \sin^2 \theta + \cos^2 \theta = 1$$

You can make use of the identities above to solve some trigonometric equations.

E X A M P L E 2

Solve the equation $2 \sin^2 x = 3 \cos x$ for $0 \leqslant x \leqslant 2\pi$.

S O L U T I O N

$2 \sin^2 x = 3 \cos x$

$\Rightarrow 2(1 - \cos^2 x) = 3 \cos x$ (replace $\sin^2 x$ with $1 - \cos^2 x$)

$\Rightarrow 2 - 2 \cos^2 x = 3 \cos x$

$\Rightarrow 2 \cos^2 x + 3 \cos x - 2 = 0$ (rearrange and note that this is a quadratic equation of the form $2c^2 + 3c - 2 = 0$ with $c = \cos x$)

$\Rightarrow (2 \cos x - 1)(\cos x + 2) = 0$ (factorising to give $(2c - 1)(c + 2) = 0$)

$\Rightarrow \cos x = \frac{1}{2}$ or $\cos x = -2$ ($\cos x = -2$ gives no solutions)

$\Rightarrow x = \dfrac{\pi}{3}$ or $\dfrac{5\pi}{3}$ in the range $0 \leqslant x \leqslant 2\pi$

Sketch the graphs of $y = 2 \sin^2 x$ and $y = 3 \cos x$ to verify that these are sensible solutions.

EXAMPLE 3

Solve the equation $3 \sin \theta = 4 \cos \theta$ for $0 \leqslant x \leqslant 360°$

SOLUTION

$$\frac{3 \sin \theta}{\cos \theta} = 4 \qquad \text{(dividing both sides by } \cos \theta\text{)}$$

$$\Rightarrow \quad 3 \tan \theta = 4 \qquad \text{(using } \frac{\sin \theta}{\cos \theta} = \tan \theta\text{)}$$

$$\Rightarrow \quad \tan \theta = \frac{4}{3} = 1.33$$

$$\Rightarrow \qquad \theta = 53.1° \text{ or } 233.1°$$

EXERCISE 3

1   (a) By replacing $\sin^2 x$ by $1 - \cos^2 x$, show that the equation
         $1 + \cos x = 3 \sin^2 x$ is equivalent to $3 \cos^2 x + \cos x - 2 = 0$.

    (b) By writing $c = \cos x$, factorise the left-hand side of this equation.

    (c) Solve the equation to find all values of x between $0°$ and $360°$.

2   Solve the following equations for $0° \leqslant \theta \leqslant 360°$.

    (a) $3 \sin \theta = 2 \cos \theta$

    (b) $0.5 \sin \theta = 0.8 \cos \theta$

    (c) $5 \sin 2\theta = 7 \cos 2\theta$

3   Solve the following equations for $0 \leqslant \theta \leqslant 2\pi$.

    (a) $2 \cos^2 \theta = \cos \theta + 1$

    (b) $\sin \theta - \sqrt{3} \cos \theta = 0$

    (c) $8 \sin^2 \theta = 7 - 2 \cos \theta$

4E A cyclist, C, cycles around a circular track,
    centre O and of radius 100 m. A photographer
    is at P, 30 m from the edge of the track.

    (a) If angle COP $= \theta$ show that
         $PC^2 = (100 \sin \theta)^2 + (130 - 100 \cos \theta)^2$.

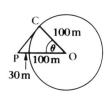

    (b) Hence show that PC $= \sqrt{(26\,900 - 26\,000 \cos \theta)}$.

    (c) If the photographer has a lens which can focus on objects at between 30 m
         and 70 m, for what range of values of θ is he able to take photographs?

1.4 $r \sin(\theta + \alpha)$

In the last section you saw how to solve equations of the form $a \sin \theta = b \cos \theta$. This section looks at equations of the form $a \sin \theta + b \cos \theta = c$.

Two men are trying to carry a wardrobe through a doorway which is too low to allow them to carry it upright. The wardrobe is 2.5 metres high and 1.5 metres wide and the doorway is 2 metres high. If the men tip the wardrobe, as shown in the diagram, they will be able to carry it through the doorway.

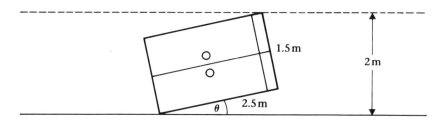

Explain why

$$2.5 \sin \theta + 1.5 \cos \theta \leqslant 2$$

if the wardrobe is to go through the doorway.

You do not yet know how to solve the equation $2.5 \sin \theta + 1.5 \cos \theta = 2$ using analytic methods. In the next tasksheet you will look at alternative ways of writing this equation in order to solve it.

TASKSHEET 3 — $a \sin \theta + b \cos \theta$ (page 27)

The expression $a \sin \theta + b \cos \theta$ is equivalent to the expression $r \sin (\theta + \alpha)$ where r and α can be found from the triangle

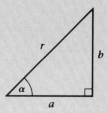

$$r = \sqrt{(a^2 + b^2)} \quad \text{and} \quad \alpha = \tan^{-1} \frac{b}{a}$$

$r \sin (\theta + \alpha)$ is a sine wave, amplitude r, phase-shifted by α in the negative x-direction.

E X A M P L E 4

Solve the equation

$$6 \sin \theta + 9 \cos \theta = 7$$

for values of θ in the range $0° \leqslant \theta \leqslant 360°$.

S O L U T I O N

$6 \sin \theta + 9 \cos \theta$ is equivalent to the expression $r \sin (\theta + \alpha)$, where r and α are found from the triangle shown below.

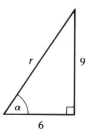

$$r = \sqrt{(6^2 + 9^2)} = 10.82 \quad \text{and} \quad \alpha = \tan^{-1} \tfrac{9}{6} = 56.31°$$

So,

$$6 \sin \theta + 9 \cos \theta = 10.82 \sin (\theta + 56.31)$$

$$\Rightarrow \quad 10.82 \sin (\theta + 56.31) = 7$$
$$\Rightarrow \qquad \sin (\theta + 56.31) = 0.6472$$

Solving the equation $\sin x = 0.6472$, where $x = \theta + 56.31$, gives $x = 40.33°$.

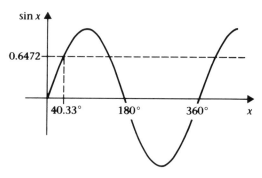

From the sketch graph, you can see that other solutions are

$x = 139.67°, 400.33°, 499.67°$, etc.

Since $x = \theta + 56.31$,

$\theta = 83.4°, 344.0°, 443.4°$, etc.

The solutions in the range $0° \leq \theta \leq 360°$ are

$\theta = 83.4°, 344.0°$ correct to 1 decimal place

EXERCISE 4

1 (a) Express $3 \sin \theta + 2 \cos \theta$ in the form $r \sin (\theta + \alpha)$.

(b) Solve the equation $3 \sin \theta + 2 \cos \theta = 3$ for $0° \leq \theta \leq 90°$.

2 (a) Explain why the maximum value of $5 \sin \theta + 12 \cos \theta$ is 13.

(b) Solve the equation $5 \sin \theta + 12 \cos \theta = 9$ for $0° \leq \theta \leq 360°$.

3

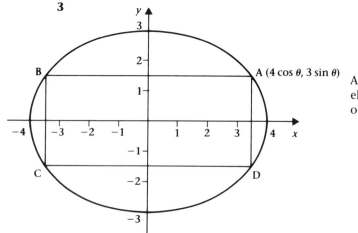

Any point on the ellipse has coordinates of the form
$(4 \cos \theta, 3 \sin \theta)$

(a) In terms of θ what are the lengths of

(i) AD   (ii) AB   (iii) the perimeter of the rectangle ABCD?

(b) If the rectangle ABCD has a perimeter of 14 units, explain why
$3 \sin \theta + 4 \cos \theta = 3.5$.

(c) Solve the equation $3 \sin \theta + 4 \cos \theta = 3.5$ and hence find the lengths of sides of the rectangle whose perimeter is 14.

(d) What is the largest possible perimeter, and for what value of θ does it occur?

4E The octopus ride is a common feature of fun-fairs. There are various designs: the one illustrated moves in a combination of horizontal circles.

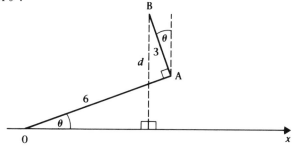

The diagram below shows the position after the arm has moved through an angle of $\theta°$.

To simplify matters, assume that the arm rotates about O, but that the chairs (at B etc.) do not rotate about A.

(a) Explain why the chair at B will move in a circle, and find the centre and radius of this circle.

(b) Calculate, in terms of θ, the distance, d, of B from the x-axis.

(c) Write the expression for d in the form $r \sin (\theta + a)$.

(d) For what value of θ is the chair at B furthest from the x-axis?

TASKSHEET 4E – Extending the method (page 29)

1.5 Addition formulas

In the last section, you considered the use of the expression $r \sin(\theta + \alpha)$. This section is concerned with general formulas for the sine and cosine of the sums of angles. Consider a rotated rectangle with a diagonal of length 1 unit.

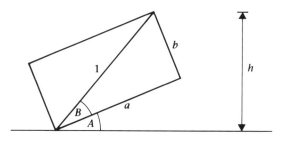

(a) Use the diagram to explain why
$\sin(A + B) = a \sin A + b \cos A$. Hence obtain the expansion

$$\sin(A + B) = \sin A \cos B + \cos A \sin B$$

(b) Similarly, explain why $\cos(A + B) = a \cos A - b \sin A$. Hence show that

$$\cos(A + B) = \cos A \cos B - \sin A \sin B$$

(c) Use your answers to (a) and (b) to help you obtain expressions for $\sin 2A$ and $\cos 2A$.

(d) Check the identities you have obtained by substituting various values for A and B.

Formulas for $\sin(A - B)$ and $\cos(A - B)$ can be obtained from the formulas for $\sin(A + B)$ and $\cos(A + B)$ simply by replacing B by $-B$. You should familiarise yourself with the following identities:

Addition formulas

$\sin(A + B) = \sin A \cos B + \cos A \sin B$

$\sin(A - B) = \sin A \cos B - \cos A \sin B$

$\cos(A + B) = \cos A \cos B - \sin A \sin B$

$\cos(A - B) = \cos A \cos B + \sin A \sin B$

$$\cos 2A = \cos^2 A - \sin^2 A \qquad \sin 2A = 2 \sin A \cos A$$
$$= 2\cos^2 A - 1$$
$$= 1 - 2\sin^2 A$$

E X A M P L E   5

Show that $\sin\left(x + \dfrac{\pi}{6}\right) = \dfrac{1}{2}\,(\sqrt{3}\,\sin x + \cos x)$

S O L U T I O N

$$\sin\left(x + \dfrac{\pi}{6}\right) = \sin x \cos \dfrac{\pi}{6} + \cos x \sin \dfrac{\pi}{6}$$

$$= \dfrac{\sqrt{3}}{2}\sin x + \dfrac{1}{2}\cos x \qquad \left(\cos \dfrac{\pi}{6} = \dfrac{\sqrt{3}}{2} \text{ and } \sin \dfrac{\pi}{6} = \dfrac{1}{2}\right)$$

$$= \dfrac{1}{2}\,(\sqrt{3}\,\sin x + \cos x)$$

E X E R C I S E   5

1 (a) Use the formula for $\sin (A + B)$ to show that
$$\sin (x + 60°) = \dfrac{1}{2}\sin x + \dfrac{\sqrt{3}}{2}\cos x$$

   (b) Check this result using a graph plotter.

2 (a) Use an addition formula to simplify $\sin (x + \pi)$.

   (b) Explain your result graphically.

3 (a) Show that $\cos (A + B) + \cos (A - B) = 2 \cos A \cos B$.

   (b) Simplify $\cos (A - B) - \cos (A + B)$.

4 (a) By writing $\sin 75°$ as $\sin (45° + 30°)$, show that $\sin 75° = \dfrac{\sqrt{3} + 1}{2\sqrt{2}}$.

   (b) Use the method of part (a) to express $\sin 15°$ in surd form (i.e. using square roots).

5 If A and B are acute angles with $\sin A = \dfrac{4}{5}$ and $\cos B = \dfrac{12}{13}$, find $\sin (A + B)$ without using a calculator. [The Pythagorean triangles with sides 3, 4, 5 and 5, 12, 13 may be useful in finding $\cos A$ and $\sin B$.]

6E Show that $\tan\left(x + \dfrac{\pi}{4}\right) = \dfrac{1 + \tan x}{1 - \tan x}$.

7E (a) By writing $\sin 3x = \sin (2x + x)$ show that $\sin 3x = 3 \sin x - 4 \sin^3 x$.

   (b) Express $\cos 3x$ in terms of $\cos x$. Verify your answer by plotting appropriate graphs.

1.6 Solution of non-right-angled triangles: the cosine rule

To 'solve a triangle' means to find all the angles and lengths of sides in the triangle. It is easy to do this for right-angled triangles. In the rest of this chapter, methods for other triangles will be considered.

LUXURY PLEASURE CRUISER IGNORES CRY FOR HELP

At 4:35 p.m. yesterday the trawler *Poisson* left Plymouth Sound alongside the cruise liner *Archimedes*. As *Poisson* headed towards Cherbourg on a bearing of 110°, *Archimedes* left for Bilbao, Spain, setting a course of 192°. 45 minutes later, after travelling a distance of 24 km, experts believe that *Poisson* was in collision with a floating piece of debris, causing extensive damage to her hull. As she went down she broadcast a distress signal (the radio had a maximum range of 50 km). The pleasure-seeking *Archimedes*, 49 km from harbour, ignored the signal and proceeded on her

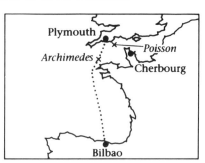

course. Within twelve minutes *Poisson* was completely submerged, and there are believed to be no survivors.

The captain of *Archimedes* has refused to comment on the incident.

Archimedes, on route for Bilbao

Do you think that the journalist was right to say that the liner *Archimedes* ignored the signal or is it possible that they were unable to hear it? (Consider an accurate plan of the course taken by the vessels.)

TASKSHEET 5 — The cosine rule (page 31)

The cosine rule for a triangle with sides a, b, c and angles A, B, C:

$a^2 = b^2 + c^2 - 2bc \cos A$
$b^2 = a^2 + c^2 - 2ac \cos B$
$c^2 = a^2 + b^2 - 2ab \cos C$

EXAMPLE 6

The hands of a clock are 10 cm and 7 cm long. Calculate the distance between their tips at 2 o'clock.

SOLUTION

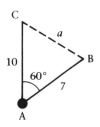

The angle between the hands is $60°$. Using the cosine rule with the triangle labelled as shown:

$a^2 = 10^2 + 7^2 - 2 \times 10 \times 7 \times \cos 60°$
$\quad = 100 + 49 - 70$
$\quad = 79$
$a = \sqrt{79} = 8.9 \text{ cm (to 1 decimal place)}$

EXERCISE 6

1   Triangle ABC is such that AB = 4 cm, AC = 8 cm and angle $A = 43°$. Calculate the length of BC.

2   (a) For triangle ABC, with sides BC = a, AC = b, AB = c, express $\cos A$ in terms of a, b, c.

(b) A triangle has sides 4 cm, 5 cm, 7 cm. Calculate its angles.

3   The hands of a clock have lengths 10 cm and 7 cm. Calculate the distance between the tips of the hands at:

(a) 4:30   (b) 8:00   (c) 6:00

4   Carry out some precise calculations to enable you to comment on the article about the liner *Archimedes*.

17

1.7 Solution of non-right-angled triangles: the sine rule

A task which is frequently given to GCSE geography students on field trips is to calculate the height of a cliff from measurements which can be taken easily, using a theodolite (an instrument for measuring angles of elevation) and a measuring tape.

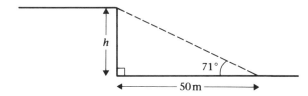

At Dover, the angle of elevation of the top of the cliff is found to be 71° from a point 50 m from the foot of the cliff.

What is the height of the cliff?

At Durdle Dor, Dorset, the beach slopes down to the sea, so that the tangent is not a useful function for calculating the height. From a point 50 m down the beach, a line to the clifftop makes an angle of 41° with the beach, as shown. The beach makes an angle of 102° with the cliff.

A method for finding the height *h* is developed on tasksheet 6.

TASKSHEET 6 — The sine rule (page 32)

The sine rule for a triangle with sides a, b, c and angles A, B, C:

$$\frac{a}{\sin A} = \frac{b}{\sin B} = \frac{c}{\sin C}$$

The area of the triangle is $\frac{1}{2} ab \sin C$

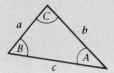

E X A M P L E   7

Solve the triangle with sides $a = 7$, $b = 12$ and angle $A = 23°$, if angle A is opposite side a.

S O L U T I O N

The first step in solving this triangle is to calculate the value of

$$\frac{a}{\sin A} = \frac{7}{\sin 23} = 17.915$$

Using the sine rule, $\dfrac{b}{\sin B} = 17.915$

and since $b = 12$, $\dfrac{12}{\sin B} = 17.915$

Rearranging this equation gives

$$\sin B = \frac{12}{17.915} = 0.670 \;\Rightarrow\; B = 42.1° \text{ (to 1 decimal place)}$$

By drawing a diagram for the triangle, show that this is not the only solution for angle B.

How many solutions are possible? What are they?

When solving triangles:

(a) Always draw a diagram as a rough check on possible solutions.

(b) Remember, there are simpler methods of solving right-angled triangles – there is no need to use the sine or cosine rule!

E X E R C I S E   7

Remember that to 'solve a triangle' means to find **all** the unknown sides and angles.

1   Use the sine rule to solve these triangles:

(a)   (b)

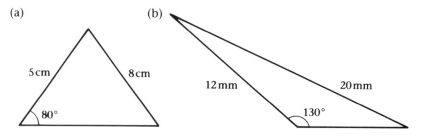

2   Use the cosine rule and then the sine rule to solve these triangles:

(a)   (b)

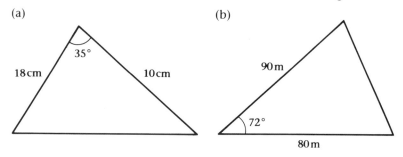

3   Find the areas of the two triangles in question 2.

4   Solve these triangles:

(a)   (b)

(c)   (d)

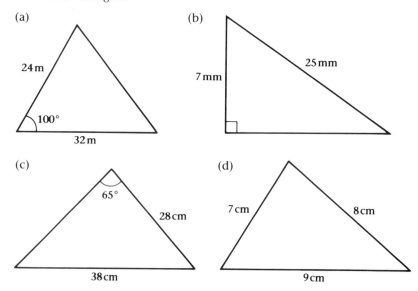

After working through this chapter you should:

1   be able to apply Pythagoras' theorem in two and three dimensions;

2   be able to find the equation of a circle or sphere, given its centre and radius;

3   know, and be able to use for simplification, the trigonometric identities

$$\tan \theta = \frac{\sin \theta}{\cos \theta}$$

$$\sin^2 \theta + \cos^2 \theta = 1$$

4   be able to find a single trigonometric function which is equivalent to $a \sin \theta + b \cos \theta$;

5   be able to solve equations of the form $a \sin \theta + b \cos \theta = c$;

6   know and be able to use the addition formulas for $\sin (A \pm B)$ and $\cos (A \pm B)$;

7   know and be able to use the double angle formulas for $\sin 2A$ and $\cos 2A$;

8   be able to solve triangles using Pythagoras' theorem, the cosine rule and the sine rule as appropriate;

9   know that the area of a triangle is $\frac{1}{2} ab \sin C$.

Pythagoras' theorem

Little is known for certain about the Greek mathematician Pythagoras. Born on the island of Samos, just off the coast of Asia Minor, around 570 BC, he travelled much throughout his life, notably in Egypt, Asia Minor and Italy. He eventually established a community of scholars at Croton, a Greek settlement in what is now southern Italy. They formed a select brotherhood sharing philosophical and political ideals as well as their study of mathematics, and lived under a strict code of discipline – temperance, purity and obedience were their watchwords. They were a secret society, and the pentagram (above) was used as a sign of recognition. Although women were forbidden by law from attending public meetings, many went to Pythagoras' lectures, and a few were even admitted to the inner circle. The Pythagoreans believed that mathematics was the key to the world. Everything was assigned a number. For example, 1 represented reason, 2 man, 3 woman, 4 justice and 5 marriage (the union of 2 and 3).

Pythagoras' influence continued after his death and his followers developed a custom of assigning all work to 'the Master' (Pythagoras). This has made it very difficult to know how much of the work assigned to him was his own, and how much his students.

It is believed that the theorem for which Pythagoras is best remembered is genuinely his work. It can be stated as

The square on the hypotenuse of a right-angled triangle is equal to the sum of the squares on the other two sides.

Pythagoras' theorem has countless practical applications in which right-angled triangles may not be immediately apparent. For example, suppose a coastguard station lying 8 km due south of the nearest airport picks up a weak radio signal from a light aircraft. The pilot reports that he is directly above a lighthouse at an altitude of 1000 m and that he only has sufficient fuel to travel a further 10 km on his current descending course towards the airport.

The coastguard telephones the airport to pass on this information, adding that she knows the lighthouse to be 3 km due east of her station. Shortly afterwards, the airport instructs the pilot to continue on his current course and make a normal landing.

This twentieth-century problem was solved using only a 2500-year-old mathematical technique.

1 Explain how the controllers at the airport made their decision as to whether the pilot should make an emergency landing. How many kilometres beyond the airport could the aircraft have flown?

Pythagoras and his students searched for sets of whole numbers which satisfied the relationship $a^2 + b^2 = c^2$. The smallest such values are 3, 4 and 5, since $9 + 16 = 25$

$$\text{i.e.} \quad 3^2 + 4^2 = 5^2$$

Sets of numbers like this are known as Pythagorean triples. Since they satisfy the relationship, any triangle with these measurements must be right-angled. This fact is still used for marking out sportsfields: a rope marked in the correct proportions and arranged in a triangle will form a right-angle.

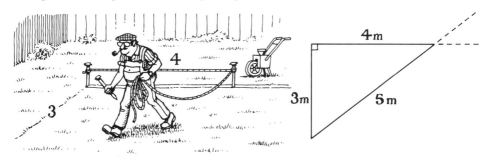

Since any triangle with these proportions must be right-angled, it follows that (6, 8, 10), (9, 12, 15) and (12, 16, 20) must also be Pythagorean triples.

The Pythagoreans could see that the hypotenuse of an isosceles right-angled triangle with two equal sides of length 1 unit would not be a whole number.

Using $h^2 = a^2 + b^2$, the hypotenuse must be $\sqrt{2}$.

You will find this triangle useful for remembering the values of the circular functions at 45°.

$$\sin 45° = \frac{1}{\sqrt{2}} \qquad \cos 45° = \frac{1}{\sqrt{2}} \qquad \tan 45° = 1$$

2 If an equilateral triangle is divided along a line of symmetry, two right-angled triangles are formed. Using half of an equilateral triangle of side 2 units, find, without using a calculator, the values of sin 30°, cos 30°, tan 30° and sin 60°, cos 60°, tan 60°. [Leave $\sqrt{3}$ in your answers.]

3 A flagpole is supported half-way up by four guy ropes, each of length 12 m. The ropes are tethered at the four corners of a rectangle measuring 5 m by 8 m. How tall is the flagpole?

4 (a) A frame is to be constructed from thirteen metal rods. Twelve of the rods are welded together to form a cuboid. The thirteenth is fitted as a crosspiece between opposite corners, thus increasing the rigidity of the structure.

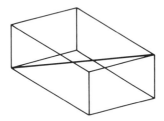

If the cuboid is made from rods measuring 18 cm, 24 cm and 11 cm, what is the length of the crosspiece?

   (b) The frames are made to a variety of sizes. If the rods used to form the cuboid measure x cm, y cm and z cm, find an expression for the length of the crosspiece.

5 Find eight Pythagorean triples which use only numbers less than 30. Group them to show which triples represent triangles with the same proportions.

Circles and spheres

A circle is made up of all the points that are fixed distance from its **centre**. The distance from the centre is the radius r of the circle.

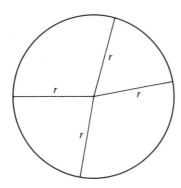

1 (a) Use Pythagoras' theorem to decide which of the following points lie on a circle with centre $(0, 0)$, radius 5:

$(4, 3)$, $(2.5, 2.5)$, $(-3, 4)$, $(-5, 0)$, $(1, -4.5)$

(b) Write down an equation connecting x and y which is satisfied by all points (x, y) which lie on this circle.

(c)* Use a graph plotter to draw the graph of this equation.

2 (a) Use Pythagoras' theorem to decide which of the following points lie on a circle with centre $(2, 5)$, radius 25:

$(27, 5)$, $(17, 25)$, $(-5, 29)$, $(-22, -2)$, $(-18, -10)$

(b) Write down an equation connecting x and y which is satisfied by all points (x, y) which lie on this circle.

(c)* Use a graph plotter to draw the graph of this equation.

3* Use a graph plotter to investigate the graph of $(x - a)^2 + (y - b)^2 = r^2$ for different values of a, b and r.

What do the constants a, b and r represent?

* For some graph plotters, you may need to rearrange the equation to give y in terms of x. This form of the equation will involve a square root, so the graph will be drawn in two sections, one part using the positive square root, and one using the negative square root.

4 A point in space can be represented by the use of three-dimensional coordinates (x, y, z). Write down the length of OP if P is

(a) $(4, 5, 6)$

(b) $(3, 0, 4)$

(c) $(-3, 0, 4)$

(d) $(-2, -1, 3)$

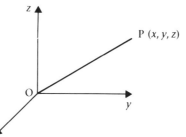

5

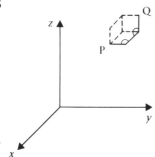

If P is the point $(3, 4, 5)$ and Q is $(6, 6, 9)$, write down the difference between their

(a) x-coordinates,

(b) y-coordinates,

(c) z-coordinates.

Hence find the distance PQ.

6 Find the distance PQ in each of the following cases:

(a) P $(5, 1, 9)$ Q $(8, 2, 3)$

(b) P $(-1, 3, 0)$ Q $(-5, -8, 1)$

(c) P (x, y, z) Q (a, b, c)

7 (a) P is a point on a sphere of radius r, centre O, with coordinates (x, y, z). Write down the length OP in terms of x, y and z and hence write down the equation of a sphere (i.e. find a relationship between x, y, z and r).

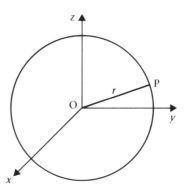

(b) Generalise the method of part (a) to write down the equation of a sphere of radius r whose centre is at the point with coordinates (a, b, c).

a sin *θ* + *b* cos *θ*

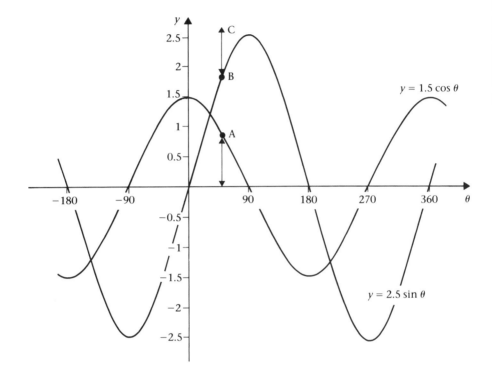

1 (a) In order to find the sum of two graphs, you may use the method of 'pointwise addition'. The value of the graph at A is added to the value at B in order to give the value at C. By adding pointwise the two graphs shown above, obtain a sketch of the graph of:

$$y = 2.5 \sin \theta + 1.5 \cos \theta \qquad \text{for } -180° \leqslant \theta \leqslant 360°$$

(b) Check your sketch using a graph plotter, and write down an approximate solution to the equation.

$$2.5 \sin \theta + 1.5 \cos \theta = 2 \qquad \text{between } 0° \text{ and } 90°$$

(c) The wardrobe in section 1.4 can be rotated through any angle between 0° and 90°.

  (i) What is the greatest height of the top corner above the ground, and for what value of θ is this height achieved?

  (ii) Through what range of angles can the wardrobe be tipped so that it fits through the door?

2 (a) Use the graph plotter to examine the graph of $y = 3 \sin \theta + 4 \cos \theta$.

(b) The resulting graph should be of the form $y = r \sin (\theta + \alpha)$. Find the values of r and α from your graph.

(c) Repeat parts (a) and (b) for one or two more graphs of the form $y = a \sin \theta + b \cos \theta$.

3 The first two questions suggest that the graph of $y = a \sin \theta + b \cos \theta$ is identical to a graph of the form $y = r \sin (\theta + \alpha)$. The diagram shows how the two expressions are connected.

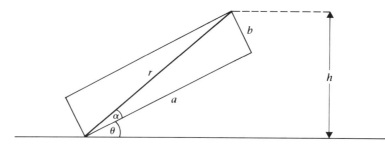

(a) Explain why

   (i) $h = a \sin \theta + b \cos \theta$

   (ii) $h = r \sin (\theta + \alpha)$

(b) Express r and α in terms of a and b.

4 (a) Use the result in question 3 to express $4 \sin \theta + 7 \cos \theta$ in the form $r \sin (\theta + \alpha)$.

(b) Verify your answer using a graph plotter.

Extending the method

The method of section 1.4, although useful, has only been developed for the expression $a \sin \theta + b \cos \theta$ on the assumption that a and b are positive. In this tasksheet, other possibilities are considered.

1

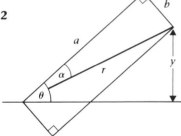

(a) Use the diagram to find an expression for x

(i) in terms of r, θ and α;

(ii) in terms of a, b and θ.

(b) Use your result from (a) to obtain an alternative expression for $a \cos \theta - b \sin \theta$.

2

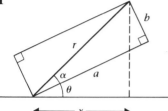

By expressing y in two different ways, explain why

$$a \sin \theta - b \cos \theta = r \sin (\theta - \alpha)$$

3 Using the diagram of question 2, explain why

$$a \cos \theta + b \sin \theta = r \cos (\theta - \alpha)$$

The expression you have just found is an alternative to the expression used in section 1.4 where you wrote $a \sin \theta + b \cos \theta = r \sin (\theta + \alpha)$.

4 (a) Express $7 \sin \theta + 4 \cos \theta$ in the form $r_1 \sin (\theta + \alpha_1)$.

(b) Express $4 \cos \theta + 7 \sin \theta$ in the form $r_2 \cos (\theta - \alpha_2)$.

(c) By plotting the two graphs show that these give the same result.

(d) What is the relationship between α_1 and α_2?

$$a \sin \theta + b \cos \theta = r \sin (\theta + \alpha)$$
$$a \sin \theta - b \cos \theta = r \sin (\theta - \alpha)$$
$$a \cos \theta + b \sin \theta = r \cos (\theta - \alpha)$$
$$a \cos \theta - b \sin \theta = r \cos (\theta + \alpha)$$

where $r = \sqrt{(a^2 + b^2)}$ and $\alpha = \tan^{-1} \dfrac{b}{a}$.

5 Express each of the following as a phase-shifted sine or cosine wave.

(a) $7 \cos \theta + 24 \sin \theta$ (b) $12 \sin \theta + 5 \cos \theta$

(c) $9 \sin \theta - 40 \cos \theta$ (d) $4 \sin \theta + 2 \cos \theta$

It is not necessary for α to be acute, although practically it is much easier to work with if it is. The next question demonstrates alternative forms.

6 This graph may be regarded either as a sine graph or as a cosine graph, phase-shifted either to the right or to the left.

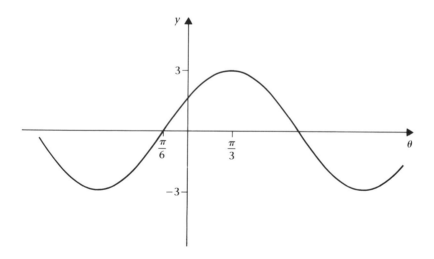

Express the graph in the form:

(a) $r \sin (\theta + \alpha)$ (b) $r \cos (\theta - \alpha)$

(c) $r \sin (\theta - \alpha)$ (d) $r \cos (\theta + \alpha)$

The cosine rule

A triangle with sides a, b, c and angles A, B, C can be divided into two right-angled triangles:

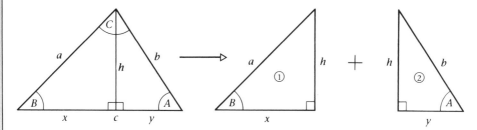

From triangle ①, Pythagoras' theorem gives

$$a^2 = h^2 + x^2$$

1 From triangle ②, express both h and y in terms of b and angle A.

2 Explain why $x = c - y$. Using this and the previous result, express x in terms of b, c and angle A.

3 Replace h and x in $a^2 = h^2 + x^2$ by the expressions found for h and x in terms of b, c and A.

4 Simplify the expression for a^2 found in question 3 by multiplying out the brackets and using the fact that $\cos^2 A + \sin^2 A = 1$.

The result is known as the **cosine rule** for triangles.

5 How does the cosine rule relate to Pythagoras' theorem for right-angled triangles?

6 By treating side b as the base of the triangle and using properties of symmetry, find a similar expression for

(a) c^2 (b) b^2

7 So far, you have only considered acute-angled triangles. How can the result be extended to obtuse-angled triangles?

The sine rule

The area of a triangle can be found using area $= \frac{1}{2} \times$ base $\times$ height.

Complete the following:

1 In the triangle with sides a, b, c and angles A, B, C as shown, the height h_1 can be expressed as

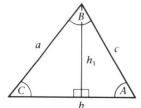

$h_1 = \underline{\quad} \sin A$

Thus the area of the triangle is

$\frac{1}{2}bh_1 = \underline{\qquad}$

2 Treating a as the base, the height h_2 of the triangle can be expressed as

$h_2 = b \sin \underline{\quad}$

Thus the area of the triangle is $\frac{1}{2}ah_2 = \underline{\qquad}$

3 Use these two expressions for the area of the triangle to form an equation. Simplify it and write it in the form $\dfrac{a}{\sin A} = \underline{\qquad}$.

4 Treating side c as the base, find an expression for the height of the triangle in terms of a and B, and hence find an expression for the area of the triangle.

5 Use the expression obtained in question 4 with each of the previous expressions to obtain two more equations simplified to the form

$\dfrac{b}{\sin B} = \underline{\qquad}$, $\dfrac{c}{\sin C} = \underline{\qquad}$

The result developed in question 1 is useful in its own right. Since triangles are normally described using lengths of sides and angles, the formula area $= \frac{1}{2}$ base $\times$ height cannot be applied directly. The following formula gives the area in terms of the lengths of two sides and the angle between them.

> Area $= \frac{1}{2} bc \sin A$
> $\quad = \frac{1}{2} \times$ product of two sides $\times$ sine of included angle

6 Find the area of triangle ABC such that AC $= 7\,$cm, BC $= 4\,$cm and angle $C = 30°$.

2 Vector geometry

2.1 Vectors and position vectors

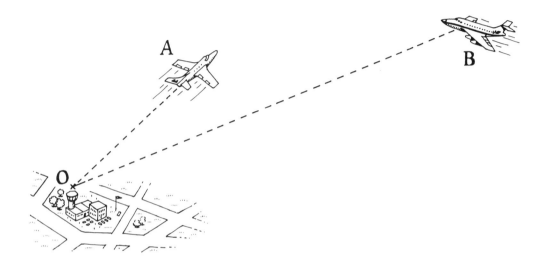

An aircraft A takes off from an airport O. After 1 minute it is 1 km east and 5 km north of O at a height of 0.8 km.

A second aircraft B is then 5 km east and 5 km north of O at a height of 4 km.

(a) What are the position vectors of the aircraft A and B one minute after A takes off?

(b) How are the vectors $\overrightarrow{OA}$, $\overrightarrow{OB}$, $\overrightarrow{AB}$ related?

(c) What are the components of the vector $\overrightarrow{AB}$?

(d) What information does the vector $\overrightarrow{AB}$ give?

Notation: The position vector $\overrightarrow{OA}$ of a point A is often denoted by $\underline{a}$ or **a**.

T A S K S H E E T   1   —   Vectors and position vectors (page 51)

33

A point may be described in terms of its **coordinates** (x, y) or in terms of its **position vector** $\begin{bmatrix} x \\ y \end{bmatrix}$, which describes a translation from the origin to the point.

For two points P and Q, with position vectors **p** and **q**, the vector describing a translation from P to Q is given by $\overrightarrow{PQ} = \mathbf{q} - \mathbf{p}$.

The **vector equation** of a line through the point with position vector $\begin{bmatrix} a_1 \\ a_2 \end{bmatrix}$ and in the direction $\begin{bmatrix} b_1 \\ b_2 \end{bmatrix}$ is:

$$\begin{bmatrix} x \\ y \end{bmatrix} = \begin{bmatrix} a_1 \\ a_2 \end{bmatrix} + t \begin{bmatrix} b_1 \\ b_2 \end{bmatrix}, \text{ where } t \text{ is a parameter}$$

Position vector of **any** point on the line

Position of a **particular** point on the line

This vector is the **direction** of the line

EXAMPLE 1

Find the vector equation of the line joining the points A (2, 3) and B (5, 4).

SOLUTION

The position vector of a point on the line is $\begin{bmatrix} 2 \\ 3 \end{bmatrix}$ and the direction of the line is given by the vector $\overrightarrow{AB} = \begin{bmatrix} 3 \\ 1 \end{bmatrix}$.

Thus the equation of the line AB is

$$\begin{bmatrix} x \\ y \end{bmatrix} = \begin{bmatrix} 2 \\ 3 \end{bmatrix} + t \begin{bmatrix} 3 \\ 1 \end{bmatrix}$$

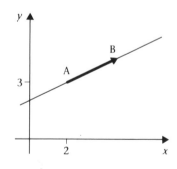

EXERCISE 1

1 Find the vector equations of the following lines:

(a) the line joining the points (4, 1) and (7, 7);

(b) the line joining the points (2, 1) and (−1, 5);

(c) the line through the point (5, 1) parallel to the vector $\begin{bmatrix} -2 \\ 4 \end{bmatrix}$;

(d) the line $y = x$;

(e) the y-axis.

2 The position vectors of four points P, Q, R and S are
$\begin{bmatrix} 3 \\ 1 \end{bmatrix}$, $\begin{bmatrix} 5 \\ -2 \end{bmatrix}$, $\begin{bmatrix} 2 \\ -4 \end{bmatrix}$ and $\begin{bmatrix} 0 \\ -1 \end{bmatrix}$.

(a) Find the vectors $\overrightarrow{PQ}$ and $\overrightarrow{SR}$.
What does this tell you about the quadrilateral PQRS?

(b) What can you say about the vectors $\overrightarrow{PS}$ and $\overrightarrow{QR}$?

3

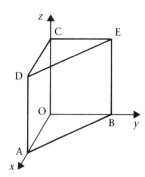

OABCDE is a triangular prism with
$\mathbf{a} = \begin{bmatrix} 6 \\ 0 \\ 0 \end{bmatrix}$, $\mathbf{b} = \begin{bmatrix} 0 \\ 8 \\ 0 \end{bmatrix}$, $\mathbf{c} = \begin{bmatrix} 0 \\ 0 \\ 10 \end{bmatrix}$

(a) (i) Find the position vectors of D and E.
(ii) Find the vectors $\overrightarrow{AB}$, $\overrightarrow{AD}$, $\overrightarrow{AC}$, $\overrightarrow{AE}$ and $\overrightarrow{DE}$.

(b) M is the midpoint of AB and N is the midpoint of DE.

(i) Find the position vectors of M and N.

(ii) Find the vectors $\overrightarrow{AN}$ and $\overrightarrow{ME}$.

(iii) Explain what you notice about the results.

4

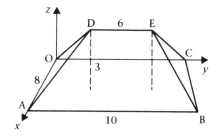

OABCDE is the roof of a house.
OABC is a rectangle with OA of
length 8 m and OC of length 10 m.
The ridge DE of length 6 m is
positioned symmetrically, 3 m
above the rectangle.

(a) With axes as shown, find the position vectors of A, B, C, D and E.

(b) Find the vectors $\overrightarrow{AD}$, $\overrightarrow{OD}$, $\overrightarrow{BE}$ and $\overrightarrow{CE}$, representing the slant edges of
the roof.

(c) What is the length of a slant edge?

2.2 Equations of lines

The ideas of section 2.1 can easily be extended to three dimensions.

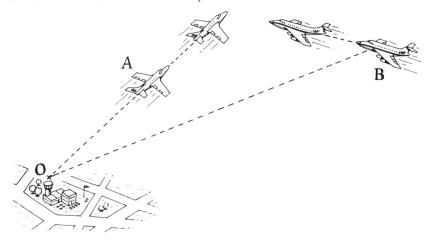

Consider the motion of the two aircraft described in section 2.1.

The position of aircraft A, *t* minutes after take-off, is given by the equation:

$$\begin{bmatrix} x \\ y \\ z \end{bmatrix} = t \begin{bmatrix} 1 \\ 5 \\ 0.8 \end{bmatrix}$$

The position of aircraft B at the same time, *t* minutes, is given by the vector equation:

$$\begin{bmatrix} x \\ y \\ z \end{bmatrix} = \begin{bmatrix} 5 \\ 0 \\ 4 \end{bmatrix} + t \begin{bmatrix} 0 \\ 5 \\ 0 \end{bmatrix}$$

(a) In what direction is aircraft B flying?

(b) Find the vector $\overrightarrow{AB}$ at intervals of 1 minute.

(c) What do you notice?

(d) How could the vector $\begin{bmatrix} 0 \\ 5 \\ 0 \end{bmatrix}$ in the equation for B

be modified to avoid calamity?

TASKSHEET 2 – Equations of lines (page 53)

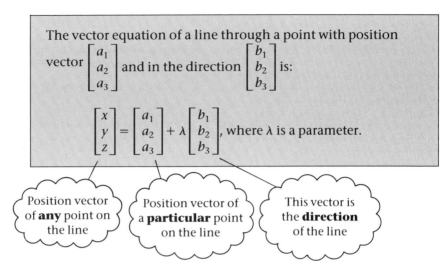

The vector equation of a line through a point with position vector $\begin{bmatrix} a_1 \\ a_2 \\ a_3 \end{bmatrix}$ and in the direction $\begin{bmatrix} b_1 \\ b_2 \\ b_3 \end{bmatrix}$ is:

$$\begin{bmatrix} x \\ y \\ z \end{bmatrix} = \begin{bmatrix} a_1 \\ a_2 \\ a_3 \end{bmatrix} + \lambda \begin{bmatrix} b_1 \\ b_2 \\ b_3 \end{bmatrix}, \text{ where } \lambda \text{ is a parameter.}$$

Position vector of **any** point on the line

Position vector of a **particular** point on the line

This vector is the **direction** of the line

[Note that the equation is often written as: $\mathbf{r} = \mathbf{a} + \lambda\mathbf{b}$]

E X A M P L E   2

Find the point of intersection of the lines with equations:

$$\begin{bmatrix} x \\ y \end{bmatrix} = \begin{bmatrix} -3 \\ 5 \end{bmatrix} + \lambda \begin{bmatrix} 2 \\ 1 \end{bmatrix} \quad \text{and} \quad \begin{bmatrix} x \\ y \end{bmatrix} = \begin{bmatrix} 4 \\ 1 \end{bmatrix} + \mu \begin{bmatrix} 1 \\ -2 \end{bmatrix}$$

> Why is it necessary to have **different** parameters, λ and μ, for the two lines?

S O L U T I O N

At the point of intersection the two position vectors will be equal.

$$-3 + 2\lambda = 4 + \mu$$
$$\text{and } 5 + \lambda = 1 - 2\mu$$
$$\text{or, } 2\lambda - \mu = 7$$
$$\lambda + 2\mu = -4$$

Solving these two equations for λ and μ gives $\lambda = 2$, $\mu = -3$ and the position vector of the point of intersection as $\begin{bmatrix} -3 \\ 5 \end{bmatrix} + \begin{bmatrix} 4 \\ 2 \end{bmatrix} = \begin{bmatrix} 1 \\ 7 \end{bmatrix}$.

> (a) Will lines in three dimensions always meet?
>
> (b) What will happen if the method of example 2 is applied in three dimensions?

EXERCISE 2

1

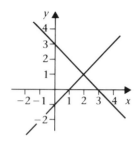

Write down vector equations for the two lines shown in the diagram.

Find the point of intersection of the two lines.

2   OABCDEFG is a cuboid with edges OA, OC and OD of lengths 4, 5 and 3 respectively.

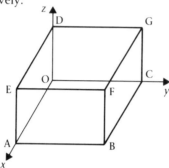

Which lines have the following vector equations?

(a) $\begin{bmatrix} x \\ y \\ z \end{bmatrix} = \lambda \begin{bmatrix} 0 \\ 5 \\ 3 \end{bmatrix}$ (b) $\begin{bmatrix} x \\ y \\ z \end{bmatrix} = \begin{bmatrix} 4 \\ 0 \\ 3 \end{bmatrix} + \lambda \begin{bmatrix} -4 \\ 5 \\ 0 \end{bmatrix}$

(c) $\begin{bmatrix} x \\ y \\ z \end{bmatrix} = \begin{bmatrix} 0 \\ 5 \\ 0 \end{bmatrix} + \lambda \begin{bmatrix} 4 \\ -5 \\ 3 \end{bmatrix}$ (d) $\begin{bmatrix} x \\ y \\ z \end{bmatrix} = \begin{bmatrix} 4 \\ 5 \\ 0 \end{bmatrix} + \lambda \begin{bmatrix} -4 \\ -5 \\ 3 \end{bmatrix}$

3   For the cuboid of question 2, find vector equations for the lines:

(a) AB   (b) AC   (c) AF   (d) AG

4   Two slant edges of a square-based pyramid, with its base on the xy plane, have equations:

$$\begin{bmatrix} x \\ y \\ z \end{bmatrix} = \begin{bmatrix} 4 \\ 3 \\ 0 \end{bmatrix} + \lambda \begin{bmatrix} -1 \\ -1 \\ 1 \end{bmatrix} \quad \text{and} \quad \begin{bmatrix} x \\ y \\ z \end{bmatrix} = \begin{bmatrix} 4 \\ -3 \\ 0 \end{bmatrix} + \mu \begin{bmatrix} -1 \\ 1 \\ 1 \end{bmatrix}$$

Find values of λ and μ such that the y and z components are equal.

Check that these values both give the same value for the x-coordinate. Hence write down the position vector of the vertex of the pyramid.

2.3 Scalar products

You are familiar with the idea of adding and subtracting vectors. This section considers one way in which a meaning can be given to multiplication of vectors.

 $\mathbf{a} = \begin{bmatrix} 3 \\ 1 \end{bmatrix}$ $\mathbf{b} = \begin{bmatrix} 2 \\ 3 \end{bmatrix}$

How could you find the angle, θ, between the two vectors?

TASKSHEET 3 — Angles between vectors (page 55)

Notation: The length or **magnitude** of the vector $\mathbf{a}$ is denoted by $|a|$, or simply by a.

> The scalar product of two vectors $\mathbf{a} = \begin{bmatrix} a_1 \\ a_2 \end{bmatrix}$ and $\mathbf{b} = \begin{bmatrix} b_1 \\ b_2 \end{bmatrix}$ is
>
> defined as $a_1 b_1 + a_2 b_2$ or $ab \cos \theta$ where a and b are the magnitudes of the two vectors and θ is the angle between them.

How would the scalar product of the following pairs of vectors be related?

(i) 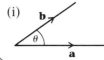   (ii) 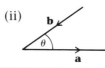   (iii)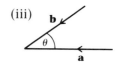

The word **scalar** is used to emphasise that the product is not a vector quantity. In fact, a second product, known as a **vector product**, exists but is beyond the scope of this unit.

The scalar product is written as $\begin{bmatrix} a_1 \\ a_2 \end{bmatrix} \cdot \begin{bmatrix} b_1 \\ b_2 \end{bmatrix}$ or as $\mathbf{a} \cdot \mathbf{b}$ which is

pronounced '$\mathbf{a}$ dot $\mathbf{b}$'. For obvious reasons some writers refer to it as the 'dot product'.

> The angle between two vectors can be found by using
>
> $$\cos \theta = \frac{\mathbf{a} \cdot \mathbf{b}}{ab}, \quad \text{where } \mathbf{a} \cdot \mathbf{b} = a_1 b_1 + a_2 b_2$$

How can the scalar product be generalised to vectors in three dimensions?

EXAMPLE 3

Find the angle between the vectors $\begin{bmatrix} 5 \\ 2 \\ -3 \end{bmatrix}$ and $\begin{bmatrix} 2 \\ 4 \\ 1 \end{bmatrix}$.

SOLUTION

By analogy with 2 dimensions,
$\mathbf{a} . \mathbf{b} = a_1b_1 + a_2b_2 + a_3b_3$
$\mathbf{a} . \mathbf{b} = 5 \times 2 + 2 \times 4 + (-3) \times 1 = 15$
$a = \sqrt{(25 + 4 + 9)} = \sqrt{38}$ $b = \sqrt{(4 + 16 + 1)} = \sqrt{21}$

So $\cos \theta = \dfrac{15}{\sqrt{38}\ \sqrt{21}} \Rightarrow \theta = 57.9°$

EXERCISE 3

1   Find the angles between:

(a) $\begin{bmatrix} 5 \\ 2 \end{bmatrix}$ and $\begin{bmatrix} 3 \\ 2 \end{bmatrix}$ (b) $\begin{bmatrix} 5 \\ 2 \end{bmatrix}$ and $\begin{bmatrix} -3 \\ 2 \end{bmatrix}$

2   In triangle ABC,   A = (3, 2),   B = (−1, 3),   C = (1, 7).

(a) Find vectors $\overrightarrow{AB}$ and $\overrightarrow{AC}$.

(b) Explain why, to calculate angle A, you should find $\overrightarrow{AB} . \overrightarrow{AC}$ and not $\overrightarrow{AB} . \overrightarrow{CA}$. Hence calculate angle A.

3   Find the angles between:

(a) $\begin{bmatrix} 12 \\ 1 \\ -12 \end{bmatrix}$ and $\begin{bmatrix} 8 \\ 4 \\ 1 \end{bmatrix}$;   (b) $\begin{bmatrix} 4 \\ -1 \\ -8 \end{bmatrix}$ and $\begin{bmatrix} 7 \\ 4 \\ -4 \end{bmatrix}$

4   In triangle PQR,   P = (5, −3, 1),   Q = (−2, 1, 5),   R = (9, 5, 0). Find the angles of the triangle.

5   If A = (2, 5, 2),   B = (3, 11 −3),   C = (7, 12, −1),   D = (6, 6, 4), show that ABCD is a parallelogram and find its sides and angles.

6E   Use the scalar product method to find the angle made by a longest diagonal of a cube with: (a) an edge of the cube;   (b) a face diagonal; (c) another longest diagonal.

2.4 Properties of the scalar product

The usefulness of the scalar product extends beyond providing a convenient method for finding the angle between vectors. Some of its properties are explored further in the next tasksheet and applied in later sections to three-dimensional geometry. Many of the properties of the scalar product are similar to those of ordinary algebra. This section examines the similarities and differences.

> What can you say about two vectors **a** and **b** if **a** . **b** = 0?

TASKSHEET 4 — Scalar products (page 56)

For the scalar product:

a . **b** = **b** . **a**

a . (**b** + **c**) = **a** . **b** + **a** . **c**

a . **b** = 0 ⇒ **a** is perpendicular to **b** or **a** = 0 or **b** = 0

a . **a** = a^2

EXERCISE 4

1 $\mathbf{a} = \begin{bmatrix} 3 \\ 2 \end{bmatrix}$ $\mathbf{b} = \begin{bmatrix} 5 \\ 3 \end{bmatrix}$ $\mathbf{c} = \begin{bmatrix} -2 \\ 3 \end{bmatrix}$

(a) Calculate the magnitudes of **a**, **b**, and **c**.

(b) Calculate the scalar products **a** . **b**, **b** . **c**, **c** . **a**.

(c) Which pair of vectors are perpendicular?

(d) Find a vector which is perpendicular to **b**.

2 $\mathbf{a} = \begin{bmatrix} 2 \\ 2 \\ 1 \end{bmatrix}$ $\mathbf{b} = \begin{bmatrix} 1 \\ 0 \\ -2 \end{bmatrix}$ $\mathbf{c} = \begin{bmatrix} 4 \\ -5 \\ 2 \end{bmatrix}$

(a) Calculate the scalar products **a** . **b**, **b** . **c**, **c** . **a**.

(b) Which pairs of vectors are perpendicular?

3 $\mathbf{a} = \begin{bmatrix} 10 \\ 0 \end{bmatrix}$ $\mathbf{b} = \begin{bmatrix} -6 \\ 8 \end{bmatrix}$

(a) Find the position vector **c** of the midpoint of AB.

(b) Find the vector $\mathbf{d} = \overrightarrow{BA}$.

(c) Calculate the scalar product **c** . **d**.

(d) Draw a diagram of the triangle OAB with the point C included. What can you deduce from the value of the scalar product **c** . **d**?

4E

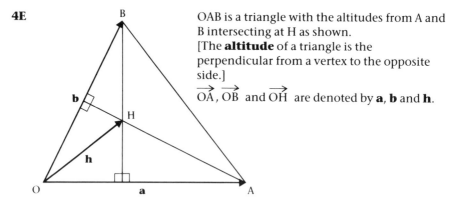

OAB is a triangle with the altitudes from A and B intersecting at H as shown.
[The **altitude** of a triangle is the perpendicular from a vertex to the opposite side.]

$\overrightarrow{OA}$, $\overrightarrow{OB}$ and $\overrightarrow{OH}$ are denoted by **a**, **b** and **h**.

(a) Why is **a** . (**b** − **h**) = 0?

(b) Write down a similar equation involving **a** − **h**.

(c) By subtracting the two equations, show that (**a** − **b**) . **h** = 0.

(d) Explain how this proves that the altitudes of a triangle are concurrent. (**Concurrent** lines all pass through a single point.)

5E   (a)

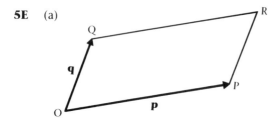

OPRQ is a parallelogram.
Write down the vectors $\overrightarrow{OR}$ and $\overrightarrow{QP}$ in terms of **p** and **q**.

(b) Explain why (**p** + **q**). (**p** − **q**) = $p^2 - q^2$.

(c) If $\overrightarrow{OR}$. $\overrightarrow{QP}$ = 0 what can you say about:

(i) the lines OR and QP   (ii) the sides of the parallelogram?

2.5 Vector equations of planes

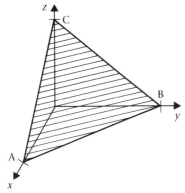

In three dimensions, as well as the equations of lines, a description of planes can be important. In describing crystals, for example, you might be interested in the various faces and the way they are related. Suppose A, B and C are three points with position vectors

$$\begin{bmatrix} 3 \\ 0 \\ 0 \end{bmatrix}, \quad \begin{bmatrix} 0 \\ 5 \\ 0 \end{bmatrix} \quad \text{and} \quad \begin{bmatrix} 0 \\ 0 \\ 4 \end{bmatrix} \text{ respectively.}$$

(a) What are the vectors $\overrightarrow{AB}$ and $\overrightarrow{AC}$?

(b) Where are the points with the following position vectors?

    (i) $\overrightarrow{OA} + \frac{1}{2}\overrightarrow{AB} + \frac{1}{2}\overrightarrow{AC}$

    (ii) $\overrightarrow{OA} + \frac{1}{4}\overrightarrow{AB} + \frac{1}{4}\overrightarrow{AC}$

    (iii) $\overrightarrow{OA} + 2\overrightarrow{AB} - \overrightarrow{AC}$

    (iv) $\overrightarrow{OA} + \lambda\overrightarrow{AB} + \mu\overrightarrow{AC}$

(c) Can **every** point in the plane ABC be found from a suitable choice of λ and μ in (b)(iv)?

TASKSHEET 5 — Vector equations of planes (page 57)

The vector equation of a plane through a point with position

vector $\begin{bmatrix} a_1 \\ a_2 \\ a_3 \end{bmatrix}$ where the vectors $\begin{bmatrix} b_1 \\ b_2 \\ b_3 \end{bmatrix}$ and $\begin{bmatrix} c_1 \\ c_2 \\ c_3 \end{bmatrix}$ are

parallel to the plane is:

$$\begin{bmatrix} x \\ y \\ z \end{bmatrix} = \begin{bmatrix} a_1 \\ a_2 \\ a_3 \end{bmatrix} + \lambda \begin{bmatrix} b_1 \\ b_2 \\ b_3 \end{bmatrix} + \mu \begin{bmatrix} c_1 \\ c_2 \\ c_3 \end{bmatrix}, \text{where } \lambda \text{ and } \mu \text{ are parameters.}$$

Position vector of **any** point on the plane

Position vector of a **particular** point on the plane

Vectors **parallel** to the plane, but not parallel to each other

The vector equation of a plane is often written in the form
r = **a** + λ**b** + μ**c**.

EXAMPLE 4

Find the vector equation of the plane through the point (2, 5, −6),
parallel to the vector $\begin{bmatrix} 4 \\ 1 \\ 3 \end{bmatrix}$ and to the z-axis.

SOLUTION

Since the z-axis is parallel to the vector $\begin{bmatrix} 0 \\ 0 \\ 1 \end{bmatrix}$, the vector equation of the

plane is:

$$\begin{bmatrix} x \\ y \\ z \end{bmatrix} = \begin{bmatrix} 2 \\ 5 \\ -6 \end{bmatrix} + \lambda \begin{bmatrix} 4 \\ 1 \\ 3 \end{bmatrix} + \mu \begin{bmatrix} 0 \\ 0 \\ 1 \end{bmatrix}$$

EXERCISE 5

1 Find a vector equation for the plane through the three points:
A (2, 3, 1), B (−1, 2, 4), C (−4, 1, 5).

2 A plane cuts the x, y and z axes at x = 2, y = −1 and z = 3. Find a vector
equation for the plane.

3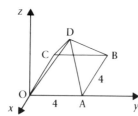

OABCD is a regular square-based pyramid with
base edges of length 4 and height 3.

(a) What is the position vector of the vertex
D?

(b) Find vector equations for the faces OAD
and BCD.

4 Explain why it is not possible to find the vector equation of the plane
through the three points A (2, 3, 1), B (−1, 2, 4), C (−4, 1, 7).

2.6 Cartesian equation of a plane

(1, 3, 0) is a point which satisfies the equation $x + y + z = 4$.
Find other points which satisfy this equation and consider
their positions in space. What does the equation represent?

The next tasksheet considers the connection between the Cartesian
equation of a plane and the vector equation.

TASKSHEET 6 – Cartesian equations of planes (page 59)

The equation $x + y + z = 12$ can be written, using scalar product
notation, as:

$$\begin{bmatrix} 1 \\ 1 \\ 1 \end{bmatrix} . \begin{bmatrix} x \\ y \\ z \end{bmatrix} = 12$$

You saw in tasksheet 6 that the vector $\begin{bmatrix} 1 \\ 1 \\ 1 \end{bmatrix}$ is at right angles to

the plane. This vector is known as the **normal vector** to the plane
and is usually written **n**. The result suggests that $\mathbf{n} . \mathbf{r} = k$, a
constant.

(a) What are the difficulties involved in talking about the
     gradient of a plane?

(b) How does the idea of a **normal vector** help in fixing the
     orientation of a plane in space?

The vector equation of any plane can be written in the form

$$\mathbf{r} = \mathbf{a} + \lambda\mathbf{b} + \mu\mathbf{c}$$

where **r** is a general point on the plane, **a** is a particular point on the
plane and **b** and **c** are two vectors parallel to the plane.

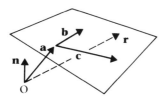

Choosing a vector **n**, which is
perpendicular to the plane, as normal
vector and considering the scalar product
$\mathbf{n} . \mathbf{r}$, you obtain
$$\mathbf{n} . \mathbf{r} = \mathbf{n} . \mathbf{a} + \lambda\mathbf{n} . \mathbf{b} + \mu\mathbf{n} . \mathbf{c}$$

(a) Why are **n** . **b** and **n** . **c** zero?

(b) Why is **n** . **a** a constant?

(c) How does this relate to the Cartesian equation of the plane in the form $ax + by + cz = d$?

The equation of a plane can be written as **n** . **r** = **n** . **a**, where **n** is a normal vector and **a** is the position vector of a point on the plane.

The normal vector to the plane $ax + by + cz = d$ is $\begin{bmatrix} a \\ b \\ c \end{bmatrix}$.

EXAMPLE 5

A plane through a point with position vector $\begin{bmatrix} 2 \\ 1 \\ 3 \end{bmatrix}$ has normal

vector $\begin{bmatrix} 3 \\ -1 \\ 4 \end{bmatrix}$. Find the Cartesian equation of the plane.

SOLUTION

Using **n** . **r** = **n** . **a**, $\begin{bmatrix} 3 \\ -1 \\ 4 \end{bmatrix} . \begin{bmatrix} x \\ y \\ z \end{bmatrix} = \begin{bmatrix} 3 \\ -1 \\ 4 \end{bmatrix} . \begin{bmatrix} 2 \\ 1 \\ 3 \end{bmatrix}$

$\Rightarrow 3x - y + 4z = 17$

EXERCISE 6

1 Find the Cartesian equations of the following:

(a) a plane through the origin with normal vector $\begin{bmatrix} 2 \\ -3 \\ 1 \end{bmatrix}$;

(b) a plane through the point $(3, 1, -2)$ parallel to the plane of part (a);

(c) a plane through the point $(3, 1, -2)$ with normal vector $\begin{bmatrix} 5 \\ -2 \\ 0 \end{bmatrix}$.

2

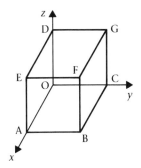

OABCDEFG is a unit cube with x, y and z axes as shown.

For each of the following planes, use inspection to write down a normal vector and give the Cartesian equation of the plane.

(a) ACGE   (b) OBFD   (c) ADC

(d) EGB   (e) OABC

3

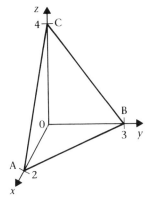

A, B and C are 2, 3 and 4 units from the origin along the x, y and z axes.

(a) What is the position vector of C?

(b) Write down the vectors $\overrightarrow{CA}$ and $\overrightarrow{CB}$.

(c) What is the vector equation of the plane ABC?

(d) Write down equations for x, y and z in terms of the parameters λ and μ.

(e) Eliminate λ and μ to find the Cartesian equation of the plane ABC.

(f) What is the normal vector to the plane ABC?

4E

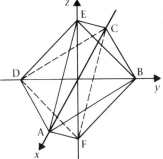

A regular octahedron ABCDEF is placed with its vertices on the x, y and z axes, each at one unit from the origin.

(a) Find the Cartesian equations of the planes AEB and DCF.

(b) What do you notice about these two planes?

(c) Find the Cartesian equations of the planes ECB and FAD.

TASKSHEET 7E — Intersections (page 61)

2.7 Finding angles

When describing a polyhedron or a crystal, it is often useful to know the angle between adjacent faces, the **dihedral** angle.

(a) When two planes intersect, which angle is considered to be the angle between the planes?

(b) How can this angle be calculated given the Cartesian equations of the planes?

EXAMPLE 6

Find the angle between

(a) the planes $3x + y - 2z = 4$ and $2x - y + 5z = 1$

(b) the plane $3x + y - 2z = 4$ and   the line $\begin{bmatrix} x \\ y \\ z \end{bmatrix} = \begin{bmatrix} 1 \\ 2 \\ 3 \end{bmatrix} + \lambda \begin{bmatrix} -1 \\ 3 \\ -5 \end{bmatrix}$

SOLUTION

(a)

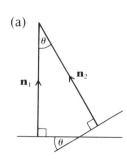

$$\mathbf{n}_1 = \begin{bmatrix} 3 \\ 1 \\ -2 \end{bmatrix} \qquad \mathbf{n}_2 = \begin{bmatrix} 2 \\ -1 \\ 5 \end{bmatrix}$$

$\mathbf{n}_1 . \mathbf{n}_2 = 6 - 1 - 10 = -5$

$|n_1| = \sqrt{(9 + 1 + 4)} = \sqrt{14}$

$|n_2| = \sqrt{(4 + 1 + 25)} = \sqrt{30}$

$\mathbf{n}_1 . \mathbf{n}_2 = |n_1| |n_2| \cos \theta \Rightarrow -5 = \sqrt{14} \sqrt{30} \cos \theta$

$\Rightarrow \theta = 104°$

The acute angle between the planes is $76°$.

(b) The direction of the line is given by the vector $\mathbf{b} = \begin{bmatrix} -1 \\ 3 \\ -5 \end{bmatrix}$

Thus the angle between the line and the normal $\mathbf{n} = \begin{bmatrix} 3 \\ 1 \\ -2 \end{bmatrix}$

is given by $\mathbf{b} \cdot \mathbf{n} = |b|\,|n|\cos\theta$
$\Rightarrow \qquad\qquad 10 = \sqrt{35}\,\sqrt{14}\cos\theta$
$\Rightarrow \qquad\qquad \theta = 63.1°$

Thus the angle between the line and the plane is
$90° - 63.1° = 26.9°$.

EXERCISE 7

1 Use the result $\cos\theta = \dfrac{\mathbf{a}\cdot\mathbf{b}}{ab}$ for the angle between two vectors to calculate the angle between the normal vectors for each pair of planes. What is the angle between the planes in each case?

(a) $x + y + z = 5$; $2x + 3y + z = 4$

(b) $x - 3y - 2z = 1$; $5x + 2z = -5$

(c) $x - 2z = 4$; $y + 3z = 6$

2 Find the angles between these pairs of lines.

(a) $\begin{bmatrix} x \\ y \end{bmatrix} = \begin{bmatrix} -1 \\ 5 \end{bmatrix} + \lambda \begin{bmatrix} 2 \\ 1 \end{bmatrix}$; $\begin{bmatrix} x \\ y \end{bmatrix} = \begin{bmatrix} 2 \\ 0 \end{bmatrix} + \mu \begin{bmatrix} -1 \\ 1 \end{bmatrix}$

(b) $\begin{bmatrix} x \\ y \\ z \end{bmatrix} = \begin{bmatrix} 1 \\ 2 \\ 3 \end{bmatrix} + \lambda \begin{bmatrix} -1 \\ 0 \\ 3 \end{bmatrix}$; $\begin{bmatrix} x \\ y \\ z \end{bmatrix} = \begin{bmatrix} 0 \\ 1 \\ 1 \end{bmatrix} + \mu \begin{bmatrix} -2 \\ 3 \\ 4 \end{bmatrix}$

3 Calculate the angle between the line

$$\begin{bmatrix} x \\ y \\ z \end{bmatrix} = \begin{bmatrix} 1 \\ -2 \\ 1 \end{bmatrix} + \lambda \begin{bmatrix} 2 \\ 1 \\ 1 \end{bmatrix}$$

and the normal vector to the plane $2x + 3y - z = 6$.
What is the angle between the line and the plane?

4 The equations of the faces AEB and ECB of the regular octahedron in question 4 of exercise 6 are:

$$x + y + z = 1 \quad \text{and} \quad -x + y + z = 1$$

Calculate the angle between the planes.
What is the dihedral angle of a regular octahedron?

5E   OABC is a tetrahedron where O is the origin and A, B, C are the points
(1, 1, 0), (0, 1, 1) and (1, 0, 1).

(a) Draw a diagram to show the tetrahedron.

(b) Calculate the lengths of the six edges to show that the tetrahedron is
regular.

(c) Find the Cartesian equations of the faces OAB and OAC and calculate
the angle between them. What is the dihedral angle of a regular
tetrahedron?

(d) Write down the vector equations of the edges BC and OA and find the
angle between them. What can be said about opposite pairs of edges of a
regular tetrahedron?

(e) Calculate the angle between the edge BC and the face OAC and use the
result to calculate the height of the tetrahedron, taking OAC as base.

After working through this chapter you should:

1   be able to use vectors in three dimensions;

2   be familiar with vector equations of lines in two and three
dimensions;

3   understand the scalar product and know its main properties;

4   be familiar with vector equations and Cartesian equations of
planes, and understand the significance of normal vectors;

5   be able to calculate angles in three-dimensional situations
involving lines and/or planes.

Vectors and position vectors

The **position vector** of a point P, relative to an origin O, is the vector $\overrightarrow{OP}$.

1 Using squared paper, draw the position vectors from the origin (0, 0) for each of the two points A and B and find the vector $\overrightarrow{AB}$ in each case.

(a) $\mathbf{a} = \begin{bmatrix} 3 \\ 2 \end{bmatrix}$; $\mathbf{b} = \begin{bmatrix} -1 \\ 2 \end{bmatrix}$ 　　(b) $\mathbf{a} = \begin{bmatrix} 2 \\ 0 \end{bmatrix}$; $\mathbf{b} = \begin{bmatrix} 3 \\ 2 \end{bmatrix}$

(c) $\mathbf{a} = \begin{bmatrix} 1 \\ -3 \end{bmatrix}$; $\mathbf{b} = \begin{bmatrix} 3 \\ 1 \end{bmatrix}$ 　　(d) $\mathbf{a} = \begin{bmatrix} 5 \\ -2 \end{bmatrix}$; $\mathbf{b} = \begin{bmatrix} 5 \\ 4 \end{bmatrix}$

2

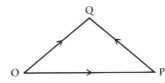

Explain why $\overrightarrow{OP} + \overrightarrow{PQ} = \overrightarrow{OQ}$.

If $\mathbf{p} = \overrightarrow{OP}$ and $\mathbf{q} = \overrightarrow{OQ}$, write down $\overrightarrow{PQ}$ in terms of $\mathbf{p}$ and $\mathbf{q}$.

3 It is not always necessary to use a square grid for vectors.

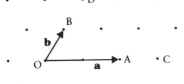

Vectors **a** and **b** are as shown on this isometric grid.

(a) Write down the position vectors of C, D, E and F in terms of **a** and **b**.

(b) Find the vectors $\overrightarrow{AB}$, $\overrightarrow{CD}$, $\overrightarrow{DE}$, $\overrightarrow{EF}$ and $\overrightarrow{FC}$ in terms of **a** and **b**.

(c) Check that $\overrightarrow{CD} + \overrightarrow{DE} + \overrightarrow{EF} + \overrightarrow{FC} = \mathbf{0}$. Why is this so?

(d) Compare $\overrightarrow{AD}$ and $\overrightarrow{EF}$. Explain what you notice.

4 On squared paper plot the points (x, y) whose position vectors are given by the following vector equations. Take 0, ±1, ±2 and ±3 as values of the parameter t.

(a) $\begin{bmatrix} x \\ y \end{bmatrix} = t \begin{bmatrix} 2 \\ 3 \end{bmatrix}$ 　　(b) $\begin{bmatrix} x \\ y \end{bmatrix} = \begin{bmatrix} 3 \\ -1 \end{bmatrix} + t \begin{bmatrix} 2 \\ 3 \end{bmatrix}$ 　　(c) $\begin{bmatrix} x \\ y \end{bmatrix} = \begin{bmatrix} 2 \\ 4 \end{bmatrix} + t \begin{bmatrix} 2 \\ 3 \end{bmatrix}$

What do you notice about each set of points?

What is the significance of the vector $\begin{bmatrix} 2 \\ 3 \end{bmatrix}$?

5 On squared paper draw the triangle OAB where A and B have position vectors

$\begin{bmatrix} 12 \\ 0 \end{bmatrix}$ and $\begin{bmatrix} 0 \\ 6 \end{bmatrix}$.

Taking 0, 1, 2 and 3 as the values of each of the parameters s, t and u in turn, draw the lines whose vector equations are:

(a) $\begin{bmatrix} x \\ y \end{bmatrix} = \begin{bmatrix} 0 \\ 6 \end{bmatrix} + s \begin{bmatrix} 2 \\ -2 \end{bmatrix}$ (b) $\begin{bmatrix} x \\ y \end{bmatrix} = \begin{bmatrix} 6 \\ 3 \end{bmatrix} + t \begin{bmatrix} -2 \\ -1 \end{bmatrix}$

(c) $\begin{bmatrix} x \\ y \end{bmatrix} = \begin{bmatrix} 12 \\ 0 \end{bmatrix} + u \begin{bmatrix} -4 \\ 1 \end{bmatrix}$

What do you notice about the three lines? Where is their point of intersection?

6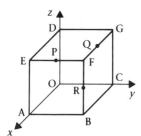

OABCDEFG is a cube with edges of length 6 and axes as shown. P, Q, R are the midpoints of the edges EF, FG and FB.

(a) Find the position vectors of the points P, Q and R.

(b) Demonstrate that $\vec{PQ} + \vec{QR} + \vec{RP} = \mathbf{0}$.

7E The vector equation $\begin{bmatrix} x \\ y \end{bmatrix} = \begin{bmatrix} 3 \\ -1 \end{bmatrix} + t \begin{bmatrix} 2 \\ 3 \end{bmatrix}$ in question 4 can be written in terms of its components as:

$x = 3 + 2t$ ①

$y = -1 + 3t$ ②

(a) Express t in terms of x from equation ①.

(b) Substitute this for t in equation ② to find the Cartesian equation of the line in the form $y = mx + c$.

(c) What is the gradient of the line? How is this related to the vector $\begin{bmatrix} 2 \\ 3 \end{bmatrix}$?

8E Find Cartesian equations for the lines:

(a) $\begin{bmatrix} x \\ y \end{bmatrix} = \begin{bmatrix} 3 \\ -2 \end{bmatrix} + s \begin{bmatrix} -2 \\ 1 \end{bmatrix}$ (b) $\begin{bmatrix} x \\ y \end{bmatrix} = \begin{bmatrix} 1 \\ -1 \end{bmatrix} + t \begin{bmatrix} 2 \\ -1 \end{bmatrix}$

Equations of lines

Questions 1 to 6 refer to the cuboid CFGEOADB with OA = 4, OB = 6 and OC = 3.

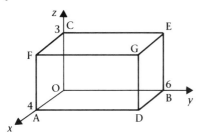

$$\overrightarrow{OA} = \begin{bmatrix} 4 \\ 0 \\ 0 \end{bmatrix}, \qquad \overrightarrow{OB} = \begin{bmatrix} 0 \\ 6 \\ 0 \end{bmatrix}, \qquad \overrightarrow{OC} = \begin{bmatrix} 0 \\ 0 \\ 3 \end{bmatrix}$$

1 Find the position vectors of the points D, E, F and G.

2 Points are given by the vector equation:

$$\begin{bmatrix} x \\ y \\ z \end{bmatrix} = \lambda \begin{bmatrix} 4 \\ 6 \\ 0 \end{bmatrix}, \qquad \text{where } \lambda \text{ is a parameter.}$$

(a) Which points correspond to $\lambda = 0$ and $\lambda = 1$?

(b) On a large copy of the diagram, mark points corresponding to $\lambda = \frac{1}{4}, \frac{1}{2}$ and $\frac{3}{4}$. What do you notice about them?

(c) What can you say about the positions of the points where $\lambda = 2$ and $\lambda = -1$?

3 $\begin{bmatrix} x \\ y \\ z \end{bmatrix} = \lambda \begin{bmatrix} 4 \\ 6 \\ 0 \end{bmatrix}$ is the **vector equation** of the line OD.

Identify the lines whose vector equations are:

(a) $\begin{bmatrix} x \\ y \\ z \end{bmatrix} = \lambda \begin{bmatrix} 0 \\ 0 \\ 3 \end{bmatrix}$ (b) $\begin{bmatrix} x \\ y \\ z \end{bmatrix} = \lambda \begin{bmatrix} 0 \\ 6 \\ 3 \end{bmatrix}$

Give vector equations for the lines:

(c) OB (d) OF (e) OG

4 Which points correspond to $\lambda = 0$ and $\lambda = 1$ on the line with vector equation

$$\begin{bmatrix} x \\ y \\ z \end{bmatrix} = \begin{bmatrix} 0 \\ 0 \\ 3 \end{bmatrix} + \lambda \begin{bmatrix} 4 \\ 6 \\ 0 \end{bmatrix} ?$$

On your copy of the diagram mark points corresponding to $\lambda = \frac{1}{4}, \frac{1}{2}$ and $\frac{3}{4}$. Where would be the points corresponding to $\lambda = 2$ and $\lambda = -1$?

5   Identify the lines whose vector equations are:

(a) $\begin{bmatrix} x \\ y \\ z \end{bmatrix} = \begin{bmatrix} 0 \\ 6 \\ 0 \end{bmatrix} + \lambda \begin{bmatrix} 0 \\ 0 \\ 3 \end{bmatrix}$ (b) $\begin{bmatrix} x \\ y \\ z \end{bmatrix} = \begin{bmatrix} 4 \\ 0 \\ 3 \end{bmatrix} + \lambda \begin{bmatrix} -4 \\ 6 \\ 0 \end{bmatrix}$

What is the significance of the vectors $\begin{bmatrix} 0 \\ 0 \\ 3 \end{bmatrix}$ in (a) and $\begin{bmatrix} -4 \\ 6 \\ 0 \end{bmatrix}$ in (b)?

The equation of a line through a point with position vector $\begin{bmatrix} a_1 \\ a_2 \\ a_3 \end{bmatrix}$ and in the

direction $\begin{bmatrix} b_1 \\ b_2 \\ b_3 \end{bmatrix}$ is:

$$\begin{bmatrix} x \\ y \\ z \end{bmatrix} = \begin{bmatrix} a_1 \\ a_2 \\ a_3 \end{bmatrix} + \lambda \begin{bmatrix} b_1 \\ b_2 \\ b_3 \end{bmatrix}$$

---

6   Give vector equations for the lines:

(a) AD   (b) AG   (c) AE

7   (a) On squared paper, draw the straight lines whose vector equations are given below by plotting points, taking $0, \pm 1, \pm 2$ as the values of the parameters λ and μ.

$$\begin{bmatrix} x \\ y \end{bmatrix} = \begin{bmatrix} 1 \\ 0 \end{bmatrix} + \lambda \begin{bmatrix} 1 \\ 1 \end{bmatrix}; \qquad \begin{bmatrix} x \\ y \end{bmatrix} = \begin{bmatrix} 1 \\ 3 \end{bmatrix} + \mu \begin{bmatrix} 2 \\ -1 \end{bmatrix}$$

(b) Where do the lines intersect?

(c) What are the values of λ and μ at this point?

(d) By equating components, write down the two simultaneous equations given by:

$$\begin{bmatrix} 1 \\ 0 \end{bmatrix} + \lambda \begin{bmatrix} 1 \\ 1 \end{bmatrix} = \begin{bmatrix} 1 \\ 3 \end{bmatrix} + \mu \begin{bmatrix} 2 \\ -1 \end{bmatrix}$$

(e) Solve the simultaneous equations and confirm your values of λ and μ.

8   Use simultaneous equations to find the intersection of:

$$\begin{bmatrix} x \\ y \end{bmatrix} = \begin{bmatrix} 2 \\ 2 \end{bmatrix} + \lambda \begin{bmatrix} 1 \\ 2 \end{bmatrix} \quad \text{and} \quad \begin{bmatrix} x \\ y \end{bmatrix} = \begin{bmatrix} 1 \\ 3 \end{bmatrix} + \mu \begin{bmatrix} 2 \\ -1 \end{bmatrix}$$

Angles between vectors

The aim of this tasksheet is to develop a particular method of finding the angle between two vectors.

1 For the triangle, $\mathbf{a} = \begin{bmatrix} 3 \\ 2 \end{bmatrix}$ and $\mathbf{b} = \begin{bmatrix} 1 \\ 4 \end{bmatrix}$.

(a) Find the magnitudes (or lengths) of vectors $\mathbf{a}$ and $\mathbf{b}$.

(b) Write vector $\mathbf{c}$ in terms of $\mathbf{a}$ and $\mathbf{b}$ and then express it as a column vector. Find the magnitude of vector $\mathbf{c}$.

(c) Use the cosine rule with your values of a, b and c (the magnitudes of $\mathbf{a}$, $\mathbf{b}$ and $\mathbf{c}$) to calculate $\cos \theta$ and find the angle θ.

The magnitude or length of the vector $\mathbf{c}$ is denoted by $|c|$ or simply c.
Similarly the magnitude of vector $\overrightarrow{AB}$ is $|AB|$ or AB.

---

2 For any triangle, $\mathbf{a} = \begin{bmatrix} a_1 \\ a_2 \end{bmatrix}$ and $\mathbf{b} = \begin{bmatrix} b_1 \\ b_2 \end{bmatrix}$.

(a) Explain why $a^2 = a_1^2 + a_2^2$ and write down a similar expression for b^2.

(b) As before, $\mathbf{c} = \mathbf{b} - \mathbf{a} = \begin{bmatrix} b_1 - a_1 \\ b_2 - a_2 \end{bmatrix}$. Since the magnitude of $\mathbf{c}$ is c, you can write:

$$c^2 = (b_1 - a_1)^2 + (b_2 - a_2)^2$$

By multiplying out the brackets and using the results of (a), show that:

$$c^2 = a^2 + b^2 - 2(a_1 b_1 + a_2 b_2)$$

(c) By comparing with the cosine rule, explain why:

$$a_1 b_1 + a_2 b_2 = ab \cos \theta$$

$ab \cos \theta$, or its equivalent, $a_1 b_1 + a_2 b_2$, is referred to as the **scalar product** of the vectors $\mathbf{a}$ and $\mathbf{b}$.

---

3 Use this result to calculate θ in question 1.

Scalar products

This tasksheet looks at some of the similarities and differences between ordinary algebra and vector algebra. Consider the vectors:

$$\mathbf{a} = \begin{bmatrix} 3 \\ 4 \end{bmatrix} \quad \mathbf{b} = \begin{bmatrix} 5 \\ 5 \end{bmatrix} \quad \mathbf{c} = \begin{bmatrix} 2 \\ 6 \end{bmatrix} \quad \mathbf{d} = \begin{bmatrix} 4 \\ -3 \end{bmatrix} \quad \mathbf{e} = \begin{bmatrix} -8 \\ 6 \end{bmatrix}$$

1 (a) Draw a diagram showing these five vectors.

   (b) Which pairs of vectors are parallel and which are perpendicular?

2 (a) Calculate the magnitude of each vector.

   (b) Calculate the scalar products: $\mathbf{a} \cdot \mathbf{a}$, $\mathbf{b} \cdot \mathbf{b}$, $\mathbf{c} \cdot \mathbf{c}$, $\mathbf{d} \cdot \mathbf{d}$, $\mathbf{e} \cdot \mathbf{e}$.

   (c) What do you notice?

3 (a) Calculate $\mathbf{a} \cdot \mathbf{b}$ and $\mathbf{b} \cdot \mathbf{a}$.

   (b) Calculate $\mathbf{a} \cdot \mathbf{c}$ and $\mathbf{c} \cdot \mathbf{a}$.

   (c) What do you notice? Explain why this occurs.

4 (a) Calculate $\mathbf{a} \cdot \mathbf{b} + \mathbf{a} \cdot \mathbf{c}$.

   (b) Calculate $\mathbf{a} \cdot (\mathbf{b} + \mathbf{c})$.

   (c) What do you notice?

5 (a) Calculate the scalar products: $\mathbf{a} \cdot \mathbf{b}$, $\mathbf{a} \cdot \mathbf{d}$, $\mathbf{a} \cdot \mathbf{e}$.

   (b) What can you say about two vectors which are perpendicular?

   (c) Find a vector which is perpendicular to $\mathbf{b}$.

   (d) Does it follow that, if two vectors have scalar product zero, then they are perpendicular?

6E

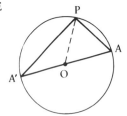

A′A is the diameter of a circle centre O and P is any point on the circumference.

(a) With $\mathbf{a} = \overrightarrow{OA}$ and $\mathbf{p} = \overrightarrow{OP}$, express $\overrightarrow{OA'}$, $\overrightarrow{AP}$ and $\overrightarrow{A'P}$ in terms of $\mathbf{a}$ and $\mathbf{p}$.

(b) Calculate $\overrightarrow{AP} \cdot \overrightarrow{A'P}$.

(c) What is the geometrical significance of the value of this scalar product?

Vector equations of planes

You will need: Datasheet 1 – *Cut-out cube*

You will need to record the results of this tasksheet for later use.

1

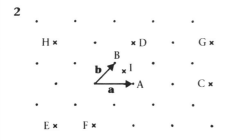

Points A and B have position vectors **a** and **b** relative to an origin O as shown.

Copy the diagram and mark on it the points having the following position vectors:

(a) $\overrightarrow{OC} = 2\mathbf{a}$ (b) $\overrightarrow{OD} = \frac{1}{2}\mathbf{b}$

(c) $\overrightarrow{OE} = 2\mathbf{a} + \mathbf{b}$ (d) $\overrightarrow{OF} = 2\mathbf{a} - \frac{1}{2}\mathbf{b}$

(e) $\overrightarrow{OG} = 3\mathbf{a} + 2\mathbf{b}$ (f) $\overrightarrow{OH} = \frac{1}{2}\mathbf{a} + \frac{2}{3}\mathbf{b}$

2

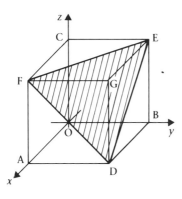

A and B are described by the position vectors **a** and **b** as shown. Express the position vectors of the points C, D, E, F, G, H, I in terms of vectors **a** and **b**.

Questions 1 and 2 illustrate that it is possible for position vectors of all points in the plane OAB to be expressed in the form $\lambda\mathbf{a} + \mu\mathbf{b}$ for some values of λ and μ. The remaining questions illustrate how this technique may be used to find the equation of any plane, not necessarily through O.

Using the cut-out from the datasheet, construct an open-topped cube with 6 cm edges and label the vertices O, A, D, B, C, F, G, E as shown.

Cut out the equilateral triangle DEF on card. Fit the triangle into the cube as shown.

The position vectors of points A, B, . . ., G are as follows:

$$\overrightarrow{OA} = \begin{bmatrix} 6 \\ 0 \\ 0 \end{bmatrix} \quad \overrightarrow{OB} = \begin{bmatrix} 0 \\ 6 \\ 0 \end{bmatrix} \quad \overrightarrow{OC} = \begin{bmatrix} 0 \\ 0 \\ 6 \end{bmatrix} \quad \overrightarrow{OD} = \begin{bmatrix} 6 \\ 6 \\ 0 \end{bmatrix}$$

$$\overrightarrow{OE} = \begin{bmatrix} 0 \\ 6 \\ 6 \end{bmatrix} \quad \overrightarrow{OF} = \begin{bmatrix} 6 \\ 0 \\ 6 \end{bmatrix} \quad \overrightarrow{OG} = \begin{bmatrix} 6 \\ 6 \\ 6 \end{bmatrix}$$

3 Find the vectors $\overrightarrow{DE}$ and $\overrightarrow{DF}$.

Explain why the position vector of any point in the plane DEF can be written as:

$$\begin{bmatrix} x \\ y \\ z \end{bmatrix} = \begin{bmatrix} 6 \\ 6 \\ 0 \end{bmatrix} + \lambda \begin{bmatrix} -6 \\ 0 \\ 6 \end{bmatrix} + \mu \begin{bmatrix} 0 \\ -6 \\ 6 \end{bmatrix}$$

This equation is known as the **vector equation of the plane**.

4 On your card triangle DEF, mark the points with the following values of λ and μ and find the coordinates of each point:

(a) $\lambda = 0, \mu = 0$ (b) $\lambda = 1, \mu = 0$ (c) $\lambda = 0, \mu = 1$

(d) $\lambda = \frac{1}{2}, \mu = \frac{1}{2}$ (e) $\lambda = \frac{1}{3}, \mu = \frac{1}{3}$

5 Cut out another equilateral triangle to form the plane ABC. What do you notice about the planes ABC and DEF?

What are the direction vectors $\overrightarrow{CB}$ and $\overrightarrow{CA}$?

Using $\overrightarrow{OC}$ as the position vector write down the vector equation of the plane ABC.

6 Repeat question 4 for the plane ABC.

7 (a) Suggest a possible vector equation for a plane parallel to ABC which passes through the origin.

(b) Likewise suggest an equation for a parallel plane through G.

8 If H is the midpoint of the line CF, find a vector equation for the plane DEH.

NB You will need to keep your cube and triangles for use with tasksheet 6.

Cartesian equations of planes

For this tasksheet you will need the open-topped cube and the triangles used for tasksheet 5, together with a knitting needle.

1

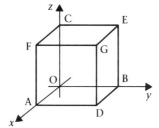

The vector equation of the plane DEF is:

$$\begin{bmatrix} x \\ y \\ z \end{bmatrix} = \begin{bmatrix} 6 \\ 6 \\ 0 \end{bmatrix} + \lambda \begin{bmatrix} -6 \\ 0 \\ 6 \end{bmatrix} + \mu \begin{bmatrix} 0 \\ -6 \\ 6 \end{bmatrix}$$

Considering the components separately, you can write the x component as:

$$x = 6 - 6\lambda$$

Write down the corresponding equations for the y and z components.

Add the three equations together and simplify. The result should involve x, y and z only and not λ and μ.

This equation is known as the **Cartesian equation** of the plane.

2 (a) What is the Cartesian equation of the plane ABC? Check your suggestion by working from the vector equation as in question 1.

In tasksheet 5 you found that this was $\begin{bmatrix} x \\ y \\ z \end{bmatrix} = \begin{bmatrix} 0 \\ 0 \\ 6 \end{bmatrix} + \lambda \begin{bmatrix} 0 \\ 6 \\ -6 \end{bmatrix} + \mu \begin{bmatrix} 6 \\ 0 \\ -6 \end{bmatrix}$.

(b) In tasksheet 5, the vector equations of the planes through O and G parallel to ABC and DEF were found to be:

$$\begin{bmatrix} x \\ y \\ z \end{bmatrix} = \lambda \begin{bmatrix} 0 \\ 6 \\ -6 \end{bmatrix} + \mu \begin{bmatrix} 6 \\ 0 \\ -6 \end{bmatrix} \quad \text{and} \quad \begin{bmatrix} x \\ y \\ z \end{bmatrix} = \begin{bmatrix} 6 \\ 6 \\ 6 \end{bmatrix} + \lambda \begin{bmatrix} 0 \\ 6 \\ -6 \end{bmatrix} + \mu \begin{bmatrix} 6 \\ 0 \\ -6 \end{bmatrix}$$

respectively. What are the Cartesian equations of these planes?

3 The vector equation of the plane DEH, where H is the midpoint of CF, is:

$$\begin{bmatrix} x \\ y \\ z \end{bmatrix} = \begin{bmatrix} 6 \\ 6 \\ 0 \end{bmatrix} + \lambda \begin{bmatrix} -6 \\ 0 \\ 6 \end{bmatrix} + \mu \begin{bmatrix} -3 \\ -6 \\ 6 \end{bmatrix}$$

Write down equations for the x, y and z components.

By eliminating λ from the first and third equations and then eliminating μ, find the Cartesian equation of the plane DEH.

4 A plane has vector equation $\begin{bmatrix} x \\ y \\ z \end{bmatrix} = \begin{bmatrix} 5 \\ 2 \\ 4 \end{bmatrix} + \lambda \begin{bmatrix} -3 \\ 0 \\ -6 \end{bmatrix} + \mu \begin{bmatrix} 2 \\ 3 \\ 1 \end{bmatrix}$.

Find the Cartesian equation of the plane.

5 The Cartesian equation of the plane DEF is $x + y + z = 12$.

Using scalar product notation, this could be written as $\begin{bmatrix} 1 \\ 1 \\ 1 \end{bmatrix} \cdot \begin{bmatrix} x \\ y \\ z \end{bmatrix} = 12$.

To investigate the significance of the vector $\begin{bmatrix} 1 \\ 1 \\ 1 \end{bmatrix}$, first note that it is in the same

direction as $\overrightarrow{OG}$, which is $\begin{bmatrix} 6 \\ 6 \\ 6 \end{bmatrix}$.

Make a hole in your card triangle DEF where OG intersects it. Pass a knitting needle through this hole and arrange it in the cube so that one end is at O.

How is this vector $\begin{bmatrix} 1 \\ 1 \\ 1 \end{bmatrix}$ related to the plane DEF?

Calculate the scalar products of $\begin{bmatrix} 1 \\ 1 \\ 1 \end{bmatrix}$ with $\overrightarrow{DE}$ and $\overrightarrow{DF}$. What do the results tell you?

6 Carry out a similar experiment for the plane DEH, using the needle to represent

$\begin{bmatrix} 2 \\ 1 \\ 2 \end{bmatrix}$ (or $\begin{bmatrix} 6 \\ 3 \\ 6 \end{bmatrix}$, which is easier to see).

(a) By eliminating λ and μ the Cartesian equation of the plane $px + qy + rz = s$ may be obtained from the vector equation of the plane

$$\begin{bmatrix} x \\ y \\ z \end{bmatrix} = \begin{bmatrix} a_1 \\ a_2 \\ a_3 \end{bmatrix} + \lambda \begin{bmatrix} b_1 \\ b_2 \\ b_3 \end{bmatrix} + \mu \begin{bmatrix} c_1 \\ c_2 \\ c_3 \end{bmatrix}$$

(b) The normal to the plane $px + qy + rz = s$ is the vector $\begin{bmatrix} p \\ q \\ r \end{bmatrix}$.

Intersections

1 Three points have coordinates:

A $(2, 2, 2)$;   B $(-1, 1, 6)$;   C $(0, 2, 5)$

(a) Find the vector equation of the plane ABC in the form:

(i) $\mathbf{r} = \overrightarrow{OC} + \lambda \overrightarrow{CA} + \mu \overrightarrow{CB}$

(ii) $\mathbf{r} = \overrightarrow{OA} + \lambda \overrightarrow{AB} + \mu \overrightarrow{AC}$

(b) Show that both vector equations give the same Cartesian equation:

$3x - y + 2z = 8$

2 Find two points which both lie on the line of intersection of the planes $3x - y + 2z = 8$ and $x - 2y + z = 1$. Hence find a vector in the direction of the line of intersection and write down the vector equation of this line.

3 By substituting for x, y and z in the equation of the plane, find the value of the parameter t at the point of intersection of the line with vector equation:

$$\begin{bmatrix} x \\ y \\ z \end{bmatrix} = \begin{bmatrix} 0 \\ 2 \\ 5 \end{bmatrix} + t \begin{bmatrix} 3 \\ -1 \\ -5 \end{bmatrix}$$

and the plane with Cartesian equation $2x + 3y + z = 7$.

Hence, write down the coordinates of the point of intersection.

4 Find the point of intersection of the three planes $x - 2y + z = 9$, $x + y + 2z = 8$, and $x - 3y + 3z = 2$.

5 What happens if you try to find the point of intersection of the three planes $x - 2y + z = 1$, $3x - y + 2z = 8$ and $4x - 3y + 3z = 5$?

In question 2, you found the direction vector of the line of intersection of the first two of these planes. In the same way, find the direction vectors of the lines of intersection of the other two pairs of planes.

How does this explain what has happened?

How are the planes related geometrically?

How is your result modified if the third equation is $4x - 3y + 3z = 9$?

3 Binomials

3.1 Binomial expansions

Algebraic expressions which have two terms, for example $a + b$, $2x - 3y$ and $p^2 + 2p$, are known as **binomials**. In the same way, an expression like $a + b + c$, with three terms, is referred to as **trinomial**.

> (a) Calculate 11^2, 11^3, 11^4.
>
> (b) What pattern do you notice?
>
> (c) What happens with 11^5?

TASKSHEET 1 — Powers of a + b (page 72)

> The binomial expression $(a + b)^n$ can be expanded using the nth line of Pascal's triangle.

EXAMPLE 1

Expand $(a + b)^n$

SOLUTION

Pascal's triangle:

$$
\begin{array}{ccccccccc}
 & & & & 1 & & & & \\
 & & & 1 & & 1 & & & \\
 & & 1 & & 2 & & 1 & & \\
 & 1 & & 3 & & 3 & & 1 & \\
1 & & 4 & & 6 & & 4 & & 1 \\
\bullet & \bullet & \bullet & \bullet & \bullet & \bullet & \bullet & &
\end{array}
$$

So $(a + b)^4 = a^4 + 4a^3b + 6a^2b^2 + 4ab^3 + b^4$

Use the method of multiplying brackets shown below to explain why Pascal's triangle generates the coefficients of powers of $a + b$.

$$(a + b)(1a^3 + 3a^2b + 3ab^2 + 1b^3) = a^4 + 3a^3b \boxed{+ 3} a^2b^2 + ab^3 +$$
$$a^3b \boxed{+ 3} a^2b^2 + 3ab^3 + b^4$$

$$\Rightarrow (a + b)^4 = \quad \ldots \boxed{+ 6} a^2b^2 \ldots$$

The result for $(a + b)^n$ can be extended to any binomial expression.

E X A M P L E   2

Expand $(2x - 3y)^3$.

S O L U T I O N

$$((2x) + (-3y))^3 = 1(2x)^3 + 3(2x)^2(-3y) + 3(2x)(-3y)^2 + 1(-3y)^3$$
$$= 8x^3 - 36x^2y + 54xy^2 - 27y^3$$

E X E R C I S E   1

1 Expand:

(a) $(a + b)^6$ (b) $(p - q)^5$

(c) $(3x + y)^4$ (d) $(1 + z)^6$

2 (a) Expand $(a + b)^3$ and $(a - b)^3$.

(b) Show that $(a + b)^3 + (a - b)^3 = 2a(a^2 + 3b^2)$.

(c) Find a corresponding result for $(a + b)^3 - (a - b)^3$.

3E (a) By putting $p = a + b$ and $q = a - b$ in question 2(b), find the factors of $p^3 + q^3$.

(b) Hence, or otherwise, factorise $p^3 - q^3$.

4E By writing 11 as $10 + 1$, explain the pattern of powers of 11.

3.2 Binomial coefficients

If a binomial expansion such as $(a + b)^3$ is expanded to give $1a^3 + 3a^2b + 3ab^2 + 1b^3$, then the coefficients are referred to as **binomial coefficients**. (For example, the binomial coefficient of a^2b is 3.)

In *Living with uncertainty*, the notation $\begin{pmatrix} n \\ r \end{pmatrix}$ was used for binomial coefficients.

r \ n	0	1	2	3	4	5
0	1					
1	1	1				
2	1	2	1			
3	1	3	3	1		
4	1	4	6	4	1	
5	1	5	10	10	5	1

(a) What are $\begin{pmatrix} 5 \\ 0 \end{pmatrix}$, $\begin{pmatrix} 5 \\ 3 \end{pmatrix}$ and $\begin{pmatrix} 5 \\ 5 \end{pmatrix}$?

(b) Why does $\begin{pmatrix} 8 \\ 3 \end{pmatrix} = \begin{pmatrix} 8 \\ 5 \end{pmatrix}$?

(c) Which other binomial coefficient is equal to $\begin{pmatrix} 10 \\ 2 \end{pmatrix}$?

(d) Why is it a sensible convention to count n and r from zero in Pascal's triangle?

It is easy enough to write down the first few lines of Pascal's triangle. However, if you want the 20th line it is a hard task to write down the preceding 19 lines! Tasksheet 2 develops a general formula for the binomial coefficients.

TASKSHEET 2 – Binomial coefficients (page 73)

The notation $n!$ (called n factorial) is used to denote

$$n(n - 1)(n - 2) \times \ldots \times 2 \times 1$$

$0!$ is defined to be equal to 1.

The binomial coefficients are then $\dbinom{n}{r} = \dfrac{n!}{r!\,(n-r)!}$

For example,

$$\binom{7}{2} = \frac{7!}{2!\,5!} = \frac{7 \times 6 \times 5 \times 4 \times 3 \times 2 \times 1}{2 \times 1 \times 5 \times 4 \times 3 \times 2 \times 1} = \frac{7 \times 6}{2 \times 1} = 21$$

Binomial coefficients may be found directly using some scientific calculators.

The binomial expansion can now be summarised in terms of binomial coefficients. The result is known as the **binomial theorem**.

For n a positive integer,

$$(a + b)^n = \binom{n}{0}a^n b^0 + \binom{n}{1}a^{n-1}b^1 + \binom{n}{2}a^{n-2}b^2 + \dots$$
$$+ \binom{n}{r}a^{n-r}b^r + \dots + \binom{n}{n}a^0 b^n$$

The series is valid for all values of a and b.

EXERCISE 2

1 Evaluate: (a) $\dbinom{8}{3}$ (b) $\dbinom{5}{2}$ (c) $\dbinom{9}{6}$ (d) $\dbinom{100}{98}$

2 Expand $(a + b)^7$ using the binomial theorem.

3 Find the first 4 terms of the expansions of:

  (a) $(a - b)^8$ (b) $(2a - 3b)^{10}$ (c) $\left(x^2 - \dfrac{1}{x^2} \right)^6$

4 If $\dbinom{15}{4} = \dbinom{15}{a}$ find a.

5 Evaluate: (a) $\dfrac{100!}{80!} \times \dfrac{78!}{99!}$ (b) $\dbinom{80}{20} \div \dbinom{80}{19}$

6E (a) Show that $\dbinom{10}{4} = \dbinom{9}{3} + \dbinom{9}{4}$.

  (b) Generalise the result in (a) and prove your result.

3.3 Binomial series

When the binomial theorem is applied to the function $(1 + x)^n$, the resulting series is particularly useful and important. Sir Isaac Newton saw that this result could be extended to powers other than positive integers. The binomial series was Newton's first major discovery, which he published in 1676 in a letter to the Royal Society.

(a) Use the binomial theorem to show that the first four terms of the expansion of $(1 + x)^n$, for n a positive integer, are:

$$1 + nx + \frac{n(n - 1)}{2!} x^2 + \frac{n(n - 1)(n - 2)}{3!} x^3 + \ldots$$

(b) How many terms are there in the whole expansion?

(c) What is the last term?

TASKSHEET 3 — Approximations (page 75)

You have seen from tasksheet 3 that the binomial expansion appears to generalise to values of n which are rational and/or negative, though with the restriction that the result only works for $-1 < x < 1$

Binomial series   For $-1 < x < 1$,

$$(1 + x)^n = 1 + nx + \frac{n(n - 1)}{2!} x^2 + \frac{n(n - 1)(n - 2)}{3!} x^3 + \ldots$$

EXAMPLE 3

Show that $\sqrt[3]{(1 - 2x)} = 1 - \frac{2}{3}x - \frac{4}{9}x^2 - \frac{40}{81}x^3 + \ldots$

SOLUTION

$$(1 - 2x)^{\frac{1}{3}} = 1 + \frac{1}{3}(-2x) + \frac{(\frac{1}{3})(-\frac{2}{3})}{2!}(-2x)^2 + \frac{(\frac{1}{3})(-\frac{2}{3})(-\frac{5}{3})}{3!}(-2x)^3 + \ldots$$

$$= 1 - \frac{2}{3}x - \frac{4}{9}x^2 - \frac{40}{81}x^3 + \ldots$$

For what range of x is this expansion valid?

E X E R C I S E   3

1 Use the formula for the binomial series to expand the following as far as the term in x^3.

(a) $(1 + x)^{\frac{1}{3}}$ (b) $(1 + x)^{-3}$

2 Use the laws of indices to write the following in the form $(1 + x)^n$. (There is no need to expand the functions.)

(a) $\sqrt{(1 + x)}$ (b) $\dfrac{1}{(1 + x)^3}$ (c) $\sqrt[5]{(1 + x)}$ (d) $\dfrac{1}{\sqrt[3]{(1 + x)}}$

3 Expand the following as far as the term in x^3.

(a) $\dfrac{1}{(1 + x)^4}$ (b) $\sqrt{(1 - 2x)}$ (c) $\dfrac{1}{\sqrt{(1 + x^2)}}$

4 (a) Explain why $\sqrt{(9 - 18x)} = 3\sqrt{(1 - 2x)}$.

(b) Show that $\sqrt{(9 - 18x)} \approx 3 - 3x - \dfrac{3}{2}x^2 - \dfrac{3}{2}x^3$, for $-\dfrac{1}{2} < x < \dfrac{1}{2}$.

5 Find the first three terms of the series expansion of:

(a) $\dfrac{1}{\sqrt{(4 + 4x)}}$ (b) $\dfrac{1}{(3 + 3x)^2}$

6 The binomial expansion for $\sqrt{(1 + x)} = 1 + \dfrac{x}{2} - \dfrac{x^2}{8} + \dfrac{x^3}{16} \cdots$

(a) Why would it be incorrect to conclude that

$$\sqrt{50} = \sqrt{(1 + 49)} = 1 + \frac{49}{2} - \frac{49^2}{8} + \frac{49^3}{16} \cdots?$$

(b) Show that $\sqrt{50} = 7\sqrt{\left(1 + \dfrac{1}{49}\right)}$ and hence find an approximate value for $\sqrt{50}$ using the binomial expansion for $\sqrt{(1 + x)}$.

7E The theory of relativity predicts that if a stick of **length l** moves with velocity v in the direction of its length it will shrink by a factor $\left(1 - \dfrac{v^2}{c^2}\right)^{\frac{1}{2}}$ where c is the speed of light.

(a) Show that for low speeds this factor is approximately $1 - \dfrac{v^2}{2c^2}$.

(b) Hence find the value of v (as a fraction of c) that makes the stick shrink to approximately $\frac{7}{8}$ths of its original length.

3.4 Error and relative error

The accuracy of a measurement depends on the instrument used for measuring. For example, using a ruler you might measure the length of a line to be between 43 and 44 mm. This can be written as 43.5 ± 0.5 mm.

6.5 ± 0.5 mm

3.5 ± 0.5 mm

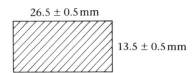

(a) What are the greatest and least possible values for

    (i) the perimeter   (ii) the area

    of the rectangles shown?

(b) (i) Express the perimeter of each rectangle in the form $p \pm e$.

    (ii) Express the area of each rectangle in the form $a \pm e$.

Expressing a result in the form $a \pm e$ is a way of stating that the result lies between $a - e$ and $a + e$. The 'error', e, measures the largest possible difference between the actual value and the number a.

E X A M P L E   4

An isosceles triangle has perimeter 72 ± 1.5 mm and base 18 ± 0.5 mm.

Express a in the form $a \pm e$.

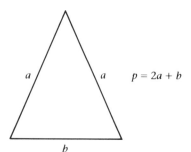

S O L U T I O N

$2a = p - b$

Maximum value of $2a = 72 + 1.5 - (18 - 0.5) = 54 + 2$ mm
Maximum value of $a = \frac{1}{2}(54 + 2) = 27 + 1$ mm
Minimum value of $2a = 72 - 1.5 - (18 + 0.5) = 54 - 2$ mm
Minimum value of $a = \frac{1}{2}(54 - 2) = 27 - 1$ mm

$a = 27 \pm 1$ mm

In example 4, the error in $p - b$ was found by **adding** the errors in p and b. The error in a was then found by **halving** the error in $2a$. These are particular cases of the following general result.

> If measurements are added or subtracted, then the errors add.
>
> $(a \pm e) + (b \pm f) = (a + b) \pm (e + f)$
> $(a \pm e) - (b \pm f) = (a - b) \pm (e + f)$
>
> If a measurement is multiplied by a precise number then the error is also multiplied by that number.
>
> $k(a \pm e) = ka \pm ke$

The next tasksheet investigates the effect of multiplying and dividing measurements.

TASKSHEET 4 – Relative error (page 77)

On the tasksheet you have seen that it can be useful to express measurements in the form $a(1 \pm r)$.

> A measurement, $a \pm e$, can be written as $a(1 \pm r)$.
>
> The quantity $r = \dfrac{e}{a}$ is called the **relative error**.

Unlike absolute errors, relative errors combine in a straightforward way when measurements are multiplied or divided.

> If measurements are multiplied or divided and if the relative errors are small, then you can add the relative errors to obtain the approximate relative error of the result.
>
> $a(1 \pm r) \times b(1 \pm s) \approx ab[1 \pm (r + s)]$
>
> $\dfrac{a(1 \pm r)}{b(1 \pm s)} \approx \dfrac{a}{b}[1 \pm (r + s)]$

EXAMPLE 5

A piece of wire, length l cm, is bent to form three sides of a rectangle.

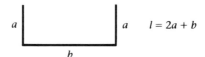

a a $l = 2a + b$

b

If $l = 20 \pm 0.4$ cm and $b = 8 \pm 0.2$ cm, calculate:

(a) the value of a (b) the area of the rectangle

SOLUTION

(a) $2a = l - b$
$$2a = (20 \pm 0.4) - (8 \pm 0.2) = 12 \pm 0.6$$
$$a = 6 \pm 0.3 \, \text{cm}$$

(b) $ab = (6 \pm 0.3)(8 \pm 0.2)$
$$= 6(1 \pm 0.05) \times 8(1 \pm 0.025)$$
$$\approx 48(1 \pm 0.075)$$
$$\approx 48 \pm 3.6 \, \text{cm}^2$$

EXERCISE 4

1 (a) Calculate the area of the rectangle in example 5 (to 1 decimal place) if the wire is bent so that $b = 19 \pm 0.2$ cm.

(b) Explain why the calculation is so inaccurate.

2 Calculate the height of the trapezium shown below if the area is 125 ± 2.5 cm^2.

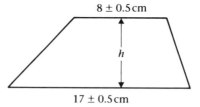

8 ± 0.5 cm

h

17 ± 0.5 cm

3 In a mechanics practical, a ball (travelling at a constant speed) is measured as travelling 50 cm in 1.32 seconds. Calculate its speed if the student can measure distance to the nearest centimetre and time to ± 0.1 second. (Give your answer in cm s^{-1} to 1 decimal place.)

After working through this chapter you should:

1   be able to use Pascal's triangle to find $(a + b)^n$ for small integral values of n;

2   know that $n! = n \times (n - 1) \times \ldots \times 2 \times 1$;

3   understand and be able to use the notation for binomial coefficients $\dbinom{n}{r} = \dfrac{n!}{r! \, (n - r)!}$;

4   be able to expand $(a + b)^n$ using the binomial theorem;

5   know how to use the binomial series and be aware of its limitations;

6   be able to calculate errors and relative errors when measurements are combined in various ways.

Powers of $a + b$

If you expand the brackets for $(a + b)(a + b)$, you obtain the identity

$$(a + b)^2 = a^2 + 2ab + b^2$$

1   Expand $(a + b)(a^2 + 2ab + b^2)$ to show that

$$(a + b)^3 = a^3 + 3a^2b + 3ab^2 + b^3$$

2   Find a similar expansion for $(a + b)^4$.

If you include the obvious results that $(a + b)^0 = 1$ and $(a + b)^1 = a + b$ and also include the (usually unnecessary) coefficient of 1, you can tabulate your results as follows:

$$
\begin{aligned}
(a + b)^0 &= & & & & \mathbf{1} & & & & \\
(a + b)^1 &= & & & \mathbf{1}a &+& \mathbf{1}b & & & \\
(a + b)^2 &= & & \mathbf{1}a^2 &+& \mathbf{2}ab &+& \mathbf{1}b^2 & & \\
(a + b)^3 &= \mathbf{1}a^3 &+& \mathbf{3}a^2b &+& \mathbf{3}ab^2 &+& \mathbf{1}b^3 & &
\end{aligned}
$$

3   (a) Can you spot the pattern produced by the coefficients of the various terms?

(b) Check whether your answer for $(a + b)^4$ fits the pattern.

(c) Assuming the pattern continues, write down what you would expect for the expansion of $(a + b)^5$.

[The answer should have six terms: a^5, a^4b, a^3b^2, a^2b^3, ab^4 and b^5.]

You should have spotted that the coefficients of the various terms are the binomial coefficients you have met before in Pascal's triangle. The pattern does continue for **all** positive integer powers of $a + b$.

4E   Find $(a + 2b)^4$.

Binomial coefficients

You can always write down the first two terms of any line of Pascal's triangle. The 10th line certainly starts 1   10, but it is not immediately obvious how to write down the next term unless you already know the 9th line.

1   The 4th line is 1   4   6   4   1. Each number is related to the previous number as shown below.

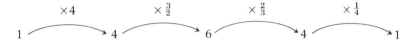

$$1 \xrightarrow{\times 4} 4 \xrightarrow{\times \frac{3}{2}} 6 \xrightarrow{\times \frac{2}{3}} 4 \xrightarrow{\times \frac{1}{4}} 1$$

How are the multipliers 4 and $\frac{3}{2}$ related to the multipliers $\frac{2}{3}$ and $\frac{1}{4}$?

2   (a) Find multipliers in a similar form for the 5th line of Pascal's triangle. (Express the multipliers with denominators 1, 2, 3, 4 and 5.)

   (b) What patterns do you notice?

3   (a) Use the pattern you have found to generate the 6th line.

   (b) Check that your result is correct by using the 5th line to generate the 6th line in the usual way.

4   Use the pattern of multipliers to generate the 10th line of Pascal's triangle.

5E   Add up the terms you have generated in question 4. How does the sum act as a check that the terms are correct?

6   Find the first four terms of the 80th line of Pascal's triangle.

The next step is to consider how any individual binomial coefficient can be found independently of any others.

Consider how the method of multipliers is used to generate the 12th line:

$$1 \xrightarrow{\times \frac{12}{1}} \frac{12}{1} \xrightarrow{\times \frac{11}{2}} \frac{12 \times 11}{1 \times 2} \xrightarrow{\times \frac{10}{3}} \frac{12 \times 11 \times 10}{1 \times 2 \times 3} \xrightarrow{\times \frac{9}{4}} \frac{12 \times 11 \times 10 \times 9}{1 \times 2 \times 3 \times 4} \quad \text{etc.}$$

$$= 12 \qquad\qquad = 66 \qquad\qquad = 220 \qquad\qquad = 495$$

Using $\binom{n}{r}$ notation, $\binom{12}{1} = \dfrac{12}{1}$, $\binom{12}{2} = \dfrac{12 \times 11}{1 \times 2}$, $\binom{12}{3} = \dfrac{12 \times 11 \times 10}{1 \times 2 \times 3}, \ldots$

7 In a similar way, write down $\binom{12}{5}$.

Results such as these can be simplified using **factorials**. For example $4 \times 3 \times 2 \times 1$ is written 4!, which is read as '4 factorial'. Most calculators have keys labelled $x!$

8 (a) By writing out the factorials and cancelling, explain why

$$\frac{12!}{7!} = 12 \times 11 \times 10 \times 9 \times 8$$

(b) Show that $\binom{12}{5} = \dfrac{12!}{5!\,7!}$.

(c) Use your calculator to evaluate $\binom{12}{5}$.

9 Use factorial notation to explain why $\binom{12}{4} = \binom{12}{8}$.

10 Evaluate: (a) $\binom{12}{9}$ (b) $\binom{12}{7}$ (c) $\binom{12}{11}$

11 Suggest a formula, using factorial notation, for $\binom{n}{r}$ in terms of n and r.

12 (a) What are the values of $\binom{12}{0}$ and $\binom{12}{12}$?

(b) How are these expressed in factorial notation, assuming that 0! has a meaning?

(c) How should 0! be defined?

Approximations

1 $(1 + x)^3 = 1 + 3x + 3x^2 + x^3$

   (a) Use a graph plotter to plot the graph of the function $(1 + x)^3$.

   (b) Plot the function $1 + 3x$, taken from the first two terms of the expansion. What do you notice about the line that is produced?

   (c) Calculate the values of $1 + 3x$ and $(1 + x)^3$ for x from 0.05 to 0.25 at intervals of 0.05. What do you notice about the results?

> $1 + 3x$ is a **linear** approximation to $(1 + x)^3$ and you will notice from your graphs and your numerical calculations that the approximation is good for small values of x.

2 (a) Compare the graphs of the functions $(1 + x)^3$ and $1 + 3x + 3x^2$.

   (b) Calculate values of $1 + 3x + 3x^2$ for the same values of x as before and compare them with the values obtained for $(1 + x)^3$ and $1 + 3x$.

> $1 + 3x + 3x^2$ is a **quadratic** approximation to $(1 + x)^3$. This is a better approximation than $1 + 3x$ for small values of x.

3 (a) Find a quadratic approximation to $(1 + x)^8$.

   (b) Use a graph plotter to compare the graph of your quadratic approximation with that of $y = (1 + x)^8$.

The binomial expansion of $(1 + x)^n$ can be written in the form

$$(1 + x)^n = 1 + nx + \frac{n(n - 1)}{2!}x^2 + \frac{n(n - 1)(n - 2)}{3!}x^3 + \ldots$$

4 (a) By putting $n = -1$ in the series above, show that a possible quadratic approximation to $(1 + x)^{-1}$ is $1 - x + x^2$.

   (b) Use a graph plotter to compare the graphs of $y = (1 + x)^{-1}$ and $1 - x + x^2$ using a domain of $-2 < x < 2$ (and $-5 < y < 5$).

   For what range of values of x is the comparison a good one?

5   (a) By putting $n = \frac{1}{2}$ into the binomial expansion, show that a possible quadratic approximation to $\sqrt{(1 + x)}$ is $1 + \frac{1}{2}x - \frac{1}{8}x^2$.

(b) Use a graph plotter to compare the graphs of $\sqrt{(1 + x)}$ and $1 + \frac{1}{2}x - \frac{1}{8}x^2$. For what range of values of x is the comparison a good one?

6   Use the binomial series to show that $1 + \frac{1}{2}x - \frac{1}{8}x^2 + \frac{1}{16}x^3$ is a possible cubic approximation to $\sqrt{(1 + x)}$. Check your result using a graph plotter.

Questions 4 to 6 suggest that the following is true for **all** values of n, provided x is small.

$$(1 + x)^n = 1 + nx + \frac{n(n - 1)x^2}{2!} + \frac{n(n - 1)(n - 2)x^3}{3!} + \dots$$

The result is known as the **binomial series**.

7E   Further evidence to support the use of the binomial series may be found by summing a geometric series.

(a) Find the sum to infinity of $1 - x + x^2 - x^3 + \dots$

(b) Expand $(1 + x)^{-1}$ from the binomial series. How does your answer relate to the sum in (a)?

Relative error

1 A rectangle has area $350 \pm 10\,\text{mm}^2$ and base $14 \pm 0.5\,\text{mm}$. Find the greatest and least possible values for the height h. Hence express h in the form $a \pm e$.

When measurements are multiplied or divided, the connection between their errors and the error in the resultant is by no means obvious. However, the binomial series can be used to show that simple connections are possible when the original measurements are in the form $1 \pm e$.

2 (a) Use the binomial series to show that, for small r,

$$(1 + r)^2 \approx 1 + 2r$$

$$\frac{1}{1 + r} \approx 1 - r$$

(b) The length of the side of a square is $1 \pm 0.05\,\text{m}$. Use the results of part (a) to find approximate bounds for

  (i) the area of the square;

  (ii) the reciprocal of the length of the side.

More generally, any two numbers of the form $1 \pm e$ can be multiplied or divided easily as is shown in question 3.

3 (a) Show that $(1 \pm r)(1 \pm s) \approx [1 \pm (r + s)]$ if rs is small enough to be ignored.

(b) By expressing $\dfrac{1 \pm r}{1 \pm s}$ as $(1 \pm r)(1 \pm s)^{-1}$, show that

$$\frac{1 \pm r}{1 \pm s} \approx 1 \pm (r + s)$$

4 Express the area in question 1 as $350(1 \pm \frac{1}{35})$ and the base length as $14(1 \pm \frac{1}{28})$. The height, h, is therefore $\dfrac{350}{14} \times \dfrac{(1 \pm \frac{1}{35})}{(1 \pm \frac{1}{28})}$.

Use the result from question 3 to write the height, h, in the form $h \pm e$. How does this compare with your answer to question 1?

4 The chain rule

4.1 Functions of functions

You already know how to differentiate polynomial functions such as $x^3 + 2x^2 - 3$ and other simple functions such as $\sin x$ and e^x. This chapter extends those methods to more complicated functions.

> A spherical balloon is being filled with air at a steady rate. How will the radius change as the balloon is being filled? Which of the graphs below is closest to what will happen and why?

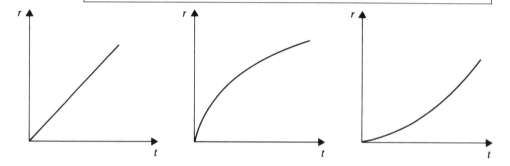

> For a spherical balloon of radius r cm, the volume in cm³ is given by
>
> $$V = \frac{4}{3}\pi r^3$$
>
> If the balloon is filled with air at the rate of 200 cm³ per second, what will be the volume t seconds after inflation is started?
>
> Combine these two equations to obtain a relationship between r and t. Sketch the graph of (t, r). Did you make the correct choice in the section above?
>
> Sketch graphs of (r, V) and (t, V).
>
> Can you think of a way to represent all three relationships in one diagram?

TASKSHEET 1 — Multicubes (page 90)

On the tasksheet you considered visual representation of algebraic relationships. Previously you have used function notation to represent such relationships.

EXAMPLE 1

If $f(x) = 3x + 7$ and $g(x) = x^3$, find $fg(x)$ and $gf(x)$.

SOLUTION

$$fg(x) = f(x^3)$$
$$= 3x^3 + 7$$
$$gf(x) = g(3x + 7)$$
$$= (3x + 7)^3$$

EXERCISE 1

1 $y = (x + 3)^3$ can be represented on a flow diagram as follows:

$$x \to \boxed{+3} \to \boxed{\text{cube}} \to y$$

Write down the expressions given by these diagrams:

(a) $x \to \boxed{-2} \to \boxed{\text{square}} \to y$

(b) $x \to \boxed{\text{sine}} \to \boxed{\times 3} \to y$

(c) $x \to \boxed{\times 2} \to \boxed{\text{exponential}} \to y$

2 Draw flow diagrams for each of the following:

(a) $2x^2$ (b) e^{3x} (c) $\sin^2 x$

3 $f(x) = 2x$ $g(x) = x^2$ $h(x) = \sin x$

If $y = fg(x)$, then $y = 2x^2$. Express the following as functions of x:

(a) $gf(x)$ (b) $gh(x)$ (c) $hg(x)$ (d) $hf(x)$

4 Choose suitable functions $f(x)$ and $g(x)$ so that each of these expressions can be written as $fg(x)$:

(a) $3x^2$ (b) $\tan 3x$ (c) $\cos^2 x$ (d) e^{x^2}

4.2 Chain rule

In this chapter you will study rates of change for **composite functions**, i.e. functions which you can think of as functions of functions. Initially, only linear relationships will be considered.

> A rod with initial temperature 50°C is being heated so that its temperature increases by 2°C per minute. What is C, the temperature in degrees Celsius, after t minutes?
>
> To convert from degrees Celsius to degrees Fahrenheit, multiply by 1.8 and add on 32. Express F, the temperature in degrees Fahrenheit after t minutes, in terms of C and then in terms of t.
>
> What are $\dfrac{dF}{dt}$, $\dfrac{dF}{dC}$ and $\dfrac{dC}{dt}$? Can you find a connection between these rates of change? Think of other examples which involve two linear functions and see if there is a similar relationship.

If z is a function of y and y is a function of x, then the relationship

$$\frac{dz}{dx} = \frac{dz}{dy} \times \frac{dy}{dx}$$

is easy to **prove** for linear functions such as $z = my + c$ and $y = nx + d$.

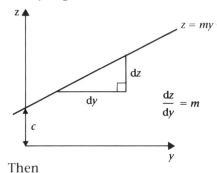

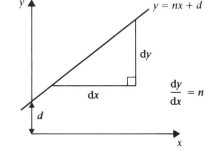

Then

$$z = m(nx + d) + c$$
$$\Rightarrow \quad z = mnx + md + c$$
$$\Rightarrow \quad \frac{dz}{dx} = mn$$

and so $\dfrac{dz}{dx} = \dfrac{dz}{dy} \times \dfrac{dy}{dx}$.

This relationship is called the **chain rule**.

If z is a linear function of y and y is a linear function of x, then to find $\dfrac{dz}{dx}$ it is not in fact necessary to first express z in terms of x. This would be especially useful if it were true generally.

$$\left(\frac{dz}{dx} = \frac{dz}{dy} \times \frac{dy}{dx} \right)$$

I wonder if this is true for non-linear functions?

> You have seen that the chain rule holds for linear functions. Why might you expect it to hold more generally?

TASKSHEET 2 — Checking the chain rule (page 92)

Linear functions are not necessary for the chain rule. Indeed, the chain rule is most useful when functions are not linear.

EXAMPLE 2

Water being poured into a paddling pool spreads at such a rate that the area in square metres covered after t minutes is $S = (5 + 4t)^2$.

(a) Find the rate at which the area is increasing after 2 minutes by multiplying out $(5 + 4t)^2$ and differentiating with respect to t.

(b) Alternatively, let $R = 5 + 4t$ so that $S = R^2$. Find $\dfrac{dS}{dt}$ by considering $\dfrac{dS}{dR} \times \dfrac{dR}{dt}$. Check that your results agree.

SOLUTION

(a) $S = 25 + 40t + 16t^2$

$\Rightarrow \dfrac{dS}{dt} = 40 + 32t$

When $t = 2$, $\dfrac{dS}{dt} = 104$

(b) $\dfrac{dS}{dR} = 2R$, $\qquad \dfrac{dR}{dt} = 4$

$$\Rightarrow \quad \frac{dS}{dt} = \frac{dS}{dR} \times \frac{dR}{dt} = 2R \times 4 = 8R$$

When $t = 2$, $R = 13$ and so $\dfrac{dS}{dt} = 104$.

EXERCISE   2

1 $S = (3 + t^2)^2$

(a) If you put $R = 3 + t^2$ it follows that $S = R^2$.

Write down $\dfrac{dR}{dt}$ and $\dfrac{dS}{dR}$ and so work out $\dfrac{dS}{dt}$.

(b) Work out $\dfrac{dS}{dt}$ by multiplying out $(3 + t^2)^2$ and check that your answer agrees with part (a).

2   You may feel that using the chain rule is not really worthwhile for differentiating $(3 + t^2)^2$. Which method would you prefer to use to find $\dfrac{dS}{dt}$ if $S = (5 + 4t)^3$?

Work out $\dfrac{dS}{dt}$ by your chosen method.

3   Work out $\dfrac{dS}{dt}$ if $S = (4 + 3t^2)^3$.

4   You have already discovered by numerical methods that the derivative of $\sin 2x$ appears to be $2 \cos 2x$.

It is possible to obtain this result using the chain rule and making a substitution for $2x$.

If $u = 2x$, then $y = \sin u$. Write down $\dfrac{dy}{du}$ and $\dfrac{du}{dx}$ and so find $\dfrac{dy}{dx}$.

5   Use the chain rule to show that the derivative of $\cos 3x$ is $-3 \sin 3x$.

6   Use the chain rule to obtain an expression for the derivative of $\sin ax$, where a is any constant.

7   Differentiate: (a) e^{3x} (b) $\sin^2 x$

The diagrams you drew in exercise 1 question 2 should help you to see which substitution to make in order to use the chain rule.

8   Differentiate: (a) e^{x^2} (b) $3 \cos 2x$ (c) $2(x^2 + 1)^3$

9 At the beginning of this chapter you considered a balloon which was being inflated at the rate of $200\,\text{cm}^3$ per second.

After t seconds, when the balloon has radius $r\,\text{cm}$ and volume $V\,\text{cm}^3$, the following formulas apply:

$$V = 200t \quad \text{and} \quad V = \frac{4}{3}\pi r^3$$

(a) Write down $\dfrac{dV}{dt}$ and $\dfrac{dV}{dr}$.

(b) By the chain rule, $\dfrac{dV}{dt} = \dfrac{dV}{dr} \times \dfrac{dr}{dt}$.

Use this to work out an expression for $\dfrac{dr}{dt}$ and so find the rate at which the radius is changing when $t = 1$.

10

When a hot-air balloon is being inflated, the balloonist finds that a good rule of thumb is that after t minutes the radius, r metres, is given by $r = 3 + 0.04t^2$. The balloon can be assumed to be roughly spherical.

(a) Work out expressions for $\dfrac{dr}{dt}$ and for $\dfrac{dV}{dr}$.

(b) Combine these two expressions to find $\dfrac{dV}{dt}$.

(c) How fast is the volume increasing after 2 minutes?

11 An ice cube is melting, and at time t hours it has the form of a cube of side $x\,\text{cm}$ and volume $V\,\text{cm}^3$.

(a) Find $\dfrac{dV}{dx}$ in terms of x.

(b) If $x = 4 - 0.5t$, write down $\dfrac{dx}{dt}$ and so find $\dfrac{dV}{dt}$.

(c) At what rate is the volume changing when $t = 2$?

4.3 Differentiation by inspection

Can you see a way of using the chain rule without showing so much working? If so, try to explain what you do when differentiating $(4x + 3)^2$ and e^{3x} with respect to x.

Expressions such as $(x^2 + 3x)^4$ and $\sin(x^2)$ can be differentiated rapidly once the stages of their composition have been recognised.

$(x^2 + 3x)^4$

$y = u^4$, where $u = x^2 + 3x$. Then $\dfrac{dy}{dx} = \dfrac{dy}{du} \times \dfrac{du}{dx}$.

The derivative is therefore:

$$4(x^2 + 3x)^3 \times (\text{derivative of } x^2 + 3x) = 4(2x + 3)(x^2 + 3x)^3$$

$\sin(x^2)$

$y = \sin u$, where $u = x^2$. The derivative is therefore:

$$\cos(x^2) \times (\text{derivative of } x^2) = 2x \cos(x^2)$$

Try to tackle the following questions by simply **writing down** derivatives whenever possible, but write out the method if you prefer.

EXERCISE 3

1 Find $\dfrac{dy}{dx}$ for each of the following. You do not need to multiply out the brackets in your answers.

(a) $y = (x^2 + 3)^4$ (b) $y = (5 + 2x)^5$

(c) $y = (2x^2 - 3x)^3$ (d) $y = (x^3 - 3x^2)^4$

2 Find the gradient of each of the following graphs at the point $(0, 1)$:

(a) $y = \cos x^2$ (b) $y = \sin 2x + 1$ (c) $y = e^{3x}$

3 Differentiate: (a) $\cos x^3$ (b) $\sin^3 x$ (c) $2 \cos^4 x$

4E Differentiate: (a) $\sin^2 2x$ (b) $3 \cos^2 4x$ (c) $e^{\sin x}$

4.4 Applications to integration

The derivative of sin $2x$ is $2 \cos 2x$. It follows that:

$$\int 2 \cos 2x \, dx = \sin 2x + c \qquad \text{and}$$

$$\int \cos 2x \, dx = \tfrac{1}{2} \sin 2x + c$$

Being able to differentiate using the chain rule greatly increases the number of functions you are able to integrate. You need to know what type of integral function you are looking for.

How can you find $\int_1^2 (5x - 3)^3 \, dx$?

E X A M P L E   3

Find $\int_0^1 (2x - 1)^4 \, dx$.

S O L U T I O N

First, try differentiating $(2x - 1)^5$.

$$y = (2x - 1)^5 \implies \frac{dy}{dx} = 5 \, (2x - 1)^4 \times 2 = 10 \, (2x - 1)^4$$

$$\text{So } \int_0^1 10 \, (2x - 1)^4 \, dx = \left[(2x - 1)^5 \right]_0^1$$

$$\implies \int_0^1 (2x - 1)^4 \, dx = \frac{1}{10} \left[(2x - 1)^5 \right]_0^1$$

$$= \frac{1}{10}[1^5 - (-1)^5] = 0.2$$

E X E R C I S E   4

1 Write down the integrals of:

(a) $\cos 3x$ (b) $\sin \tfrac{1}{2}x$ (c) $2 \sin 5x$ (d) e^{2x}

2   Find:

(a) $\displaystyle\int_1^2 e^{0.5x}\,dx$ (b) $\displaystyle\int_{-1}^0 \sin 2x\,dx$

(c) $\displaystyle\int_0^2 3\cos\tfrac12 x\,dx$ (d) $\displaystyle\int_0^1 (2x+3)^2\,dx$

3   Work out the coordinates of the points A, B and C and then evaluate the shaded areas.

(a) 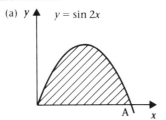 $y = \sin 2x$

(b) 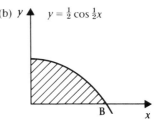 $y = \tfrac12 \cos\tfrac12 x$

(c) 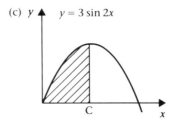 $y = 3\sin 2x$

4E   If $y = \sin x^2$, $\dfrac{dy}{dx} = 2x\cos x^2$.

Use a numerical method to check if $\displaystyle\int_1^2 \cos x^2\,dx = \left[\dfrac{1}{2x}\sin x^2\right]_1^2$.

Try to explain what you find.

5E   Some of these functions can be integrated by the methods of this section. Integrate as many of them as possible:

(a) $\cos\tfrac12 x$ (b) $e^{2.5x}$ (c) $(x^2 - 3)^3$

(d) $(5x + 3)^4$ (e) $\sin 5x$ (f) $\sin x^3$

6E   Since $\dfrac{d}{dx}(\sin x^2) = 2x\cos x^2$, $\displaystyle\int x\cos x^2\,dx = \dfrac{1}{2}\sin x^2 + c$

Find the following integrals:

(a) $\displaystyle\int x\sin x^2\,dx$ (b) $\displaystyle\int x^2 e^{x^3}\,dx$ (c) $\displaystyle\int 2x(2x^2 + 1)^4\,dx$

7E   Use the identity $\cos 2x \equiv 1 - 2\sin^2 x$ to find $\displaystyle\int_0^1 \sin^2 x\,dx$.

4.5 Inverse functions and x^n

You know how to differentiate x^2 but not the inverse of this function, $\sqrt{x}$. The chain rule enables you to find the derivative in such cases, using the fact that

$$\frac{dx}{dy} \times \frac{dy}{dx} = 1$$

(a) If y is a function of x, explain why

$$\frac{dx}{dy} \times \frac{dy}{dx} = 1$$

and $\quad \dfrac{dx}{dy} = 1 \div \dfrac{dy}{dx}$

(b) What connection is there between this result and the chain rule?

E X A M P L E 4

Find the derivative of $y = \sqrt{x}$.

S O L U T I O N

$$x = y^2$$

$$\Rightarrow \frac{dx}{dy} = 2y \Rightarrow \frac{dy}{dx} = \frac{1}{2y} = \frac{1}{2\sqrt{x}} \Rightarrow \frac{dy}{dx} = \frac{1}{2}x^{-\frac{1}{2}}$$

You already know that if n is a positive integer, then

$$y = x^n \Rightarrow \frac{dy}{dx} = nx^{n-1}$$

The working above shows that the rule is also applicable when $n = \frac{1}{2}$. In fact the result is generally true.

If $y = x^n$, then $\dfrac{dy}{dx} = nx^{n-1}$ for all values of n.

(a) Show that the derivative of $\dfrac{1}{x^2}$ is $-\dfrac{2}{x^3}$.

(b) Find the derivative of $\sqrt{x}(1 + x)$.

EXERCISE 5

1 Differentiate:

  (a) $\sqrt[3]{x}$ (i.e. $x^{\frac{1}{3}}$)   (b) $\dfrac{1}{x}$ (c) x^{-3} (d) $\dfrac{1}{x^2} + \sqrt{x}$

2 Find the derivative of $\sqrt[n]{x}$ (i.e. $x^{\frac{1}{n}}$) with respect to x.

3 The derivative of $\ln x$ is $\dfrac{1}{x}$.

  Use the chain rule to find the derivative of $\ln 2x$. (Start by putting $u = 2x$.)

4 (a) Work out the derivatives of $\ln 3x$ and $\ln 5x$.

  (b) What is the derivative of $\ln ax$, where a is any constant?

  (c) Use the laws of logarithms to explain the result above.

5 (a) Integrate $\dfrac{1}{2x}$.

  (b) What is the integral of $\dfrac{1}{ax}$ with respect to x, where a is any constant?

6E If $y = \ln x$, then $x = e^{y}$.

  Write down $\dfrac{dx}{dy}$ and use this to find $\dfrac{dy}{dx}$. Hence explain why

  the derivative of $\ln x$ is $\dfrac{1}{x}$.

7E If $y = \sqrt[3]{x}$ then $x = y^{3}$. Find $\dfrac{dx}{dy}$ and hence find $\dfrac{dy}{dx}$.

  Check that your answer agrees with that for question 1(a).

8E If $y = \sin^{-1}x$, then $x = \sin y$.

  (a) Write down $\dfrac{dx}{dy}$ and $\dfrac{dy}{dx}$.

  (b) Express the third side of the triangle
    opposite in terms of x. Hence explain why
    the derivative of $\sin^{-1}x$ is $\dfrac{1}{\sqrt{(1 - x^2)}}$.

  (c) By a similar method, find the derivative of $\cos^{-1}x$.

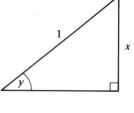

9E For the balloon problem at the start of the chapter you found that

$$r = \sqrt[3]{\left(\frac{150t}{\pi}\right)} \quad \text{or} \quad t = \frac{\pi r^3}{150}$$

Work out $\dfrac{\mathrm{d}r}{\mathrm{d}t}$ from one (or both!) of these expressions.

Does your answer agree with that to question 9 (b) of exercise 2?

After working through this chapter you should:

1 know how to use the chain rule to solve problems involving rates of change;

2 be able to differentiate functions of functions such as $(3x^2 + 5)^3$ and $\sin^2 x$;

3 be aware that the relationship

$$\frac{\mathrm{d}}{\mathrm{d}x}(x^n) = nx^{n-1}$$

appears to hold even for non-integer values of n;

4 know how to differentiate inverse functions using the fact that

$$\frac{\mathrm{d}x}{\mathrm{d}y} = 1 \div \frac{\mathrm{d}y}{\mathrm{d}x}$$

Multicubes

You will need:
Multicubes base-board and interlocking
cubes, or equivalent Lego bricks

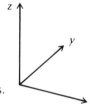

In order to represent the relationship between three
variables, you can use three-dimensional coordinates.

A model is helpful for visualising this and you can build one using a base-board and interlocking centimetre cubes.

On the base-board, consider x and y axes in the normal positions and take the bottom left-hand corner hole as $(0, 0)$. Imagine the z axis vertically upwards from this corner.

1 Consider the relationships $y = \sqrt{x}$ and $z = y + 1$.

Mark on the base-board the integral points $(0, 0)$, $(1, 1)$, $(4, 2)$ and $(9, 3)$ for $y = \sqrt{x}$.

Since $z = y + 1$, the point $(0, 0)$ should have a column 1 cube high; that for $(1, 1)$ should go up 2 cubes; and so on.

When you have built up all the columns, you can picture the three-dimensional graph for x, y and z as a curve passing through the centres of the top cubes.

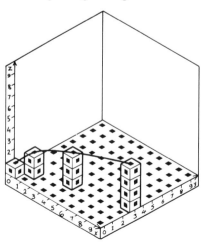

You can also see the three separate relationships by considering projections of this graph.

The (x, y) relationship is clearly visible by looking straight down onto the base-board.

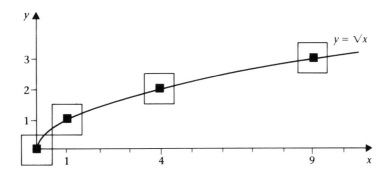

Hold up the multicube model and look straight onto the (y, z) plane. The projection of the curve onto this plane can be drawn on squared paper – you should obtain the line $z = y + 1$.

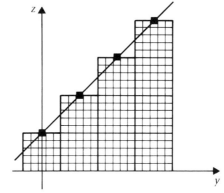

Now look straight onto the (x, z) plane and work out the projection. Combine the two given equations to obtain the relationship between z and x. Does your projection agree with this?

2   Repeat question 1 for the relationships $y = \frac{1}{3}x$, $z = y^2$.

3   It will sometimes be necessary to rescale your model. Choose sensible scales for the relationships $z = 3y$, $y = x^2$.

4   Choose scales so that you can make an approximate representation of the balloon problem of section 1.1.

Checking the chain rule

The relationship $\dfrac{dy}{dx} = \dfrac{dy}{du} \times \dfrac{du}{dx}$ is called the chain rule.

You have seen a proof of the chain rule for linear functions. Experience might lead you to expect that it is also true for any **locally straight** functions.

For example, $y = \sin x^3$ is a composite of the locally straight functions $y = \sin u$ and $u = x^3$.

If the chain rule does work for non-linear functions then:

$$\frac{dy}{dx} = \frac{dy}{du} \times \frac{du}{dx} \quad \text{where} \quad \frac{dy}{du} = \cos u \quad \text{and} \quad \frac{du}{dx} = 3x^2$$

$$\Rightarrow \quad \frac{dy}{dx} = (\cos u) \times (3x^2)$$
$$= (\cos x^3) \times (3x^2)$$
$$= 3x^2 \cos x^3$$

The example above shows that if the chain works, then

$$f(x) = \sin x^3 \ \Rightarrow \ f'(x) = 3x^2 \cos x^3$$

You can check this for any particular value of x by using a numerical method for differentiating the function and comparing it with the above formula for the derivative. Alternatively, you could use a graphical calculator or a computer to numerically differentiate the function for several different values of x and then plot the $(x, f'(x))$ points as a graph. You can then superimpose $y = 3x^2 \cos x^3$ and check that the graphs are the same.

1 Assume that the chain rule holds for any locally straight functions and use it to find $\dfrac{dy}{dx}$ if:

(a) $y = u^3$ and $u = \sin x$ (i.e. $y = \sin^3 x$)

(b) $y = e^u$ and $u = x^2$

(c) $y = u^2$ and $u = e^x$

2 Check the answers you have obtained for question 1 by a numerical method.

5 Differential equations

5.1 Introduction

A murder victim was discovered by the police at 6:00 a.m. The body temperature of the victim was measured and found to be 25 °C. A doctor arrived on the scene of the crime 30 minutes later and measured the body temperature again. It was found to be 22 °C. The temperature of the room had remained constant at 15 °C. The doctor, knowing normal body temperature to be 37 °C, was able to estimate the time of death of the victim.

What would be your estimate for the time of death? What assumptions have you made?

The cooling of an object which is hotter than its surroundings is described by Newton's law of cooling.

The rate of cooling at any instant is directly proportional to the difference in temperature between the object and its surroundings.

TASKSHEET 1 — Cooling curves (page 112)

Using calculus notation, Newton's law of cooling can be expressed as:

$$\frac{dy}{dt} = -ky$$

Explain the meaning of each of the symbols used in the formulation of the law given above.

The equation for Newton's law of cooling is an example of an equation involving a derivative. Any equation involving a derivative, such as $\dfrac{dy}{dx}$ or $\dfrac{dy}{dt}$, is called a **differential equation**.

At any point on the graph drawn below, the gradient is the negative of the y-coordinate, i.e.

$$\frac{dy}{dx} = -y$$

The graph shows the **particular solution** to the differential equation $\dfrac{dy}{dx} = -y$ which passes through (0, 1).

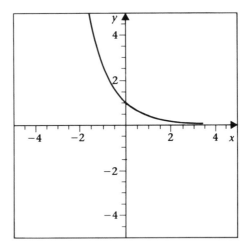

It is possible to draw other solutions, for example:

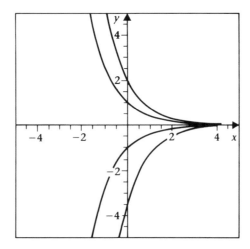

The problem of the murder victim will be solved in section 5.5.

EXERCISE 1

1   Three particular solutions of a certain differential equation are as shown.

Take suitable measurements using an SMP gradient measurer and complete the table below for the bottom curve in the graph below.

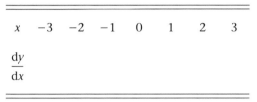

x	-3	-2	-1	0	1	2	3
$\dfrac{dy}{dx}$							

(a) Suggest a formula for the differential equation satisfied by the bottom curve.

(b) Check that all three curves satisfy the differential equation.

(c) Find formulas relating y to x for each of the three curves. What is the relationship between each formula and the differential equation you discovered in (a)?

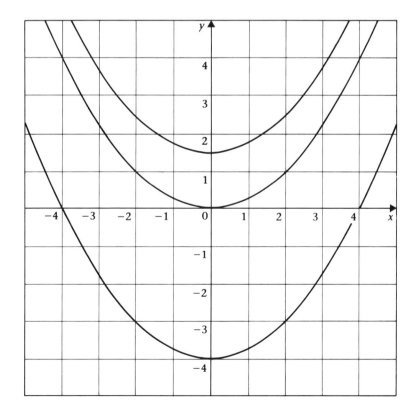

2 Five particular solutions of a certain differential equation have been sketched as shown.

The table below contains approximate measurements for the bottom curve.

x	-3	-2	-1	0
y	-0.8	-1.3	-2.1	-3.5
$\dfrac{dy}{dx}$	-0.4	-0.6	-1.1	-1.8

(a) Suggest a formula for the differential equation satisfied by the bottom curve.

(b) Using the SMP gradient measurer, complete a similar table for the curve through the point $(0, 1)$. Making allowance for errors in measurements, does it agree with your suggested formula?

(c) Measure the gradient for the four top curves where $y = 3$. Do all these results agree with your formula?

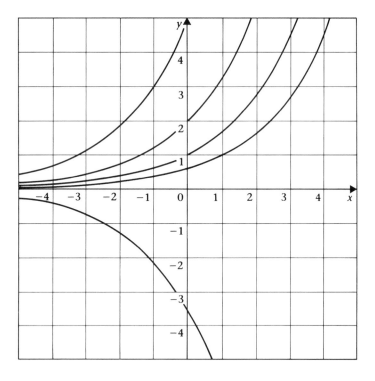

5.2 Algebraic solutions

Some differential equations can be solved algebraically by inspection. For example, if you know that $\dfrac{dy}{dx} = x^2$, then integrating the function gives $y = \dfrac{1}{3}x^3 + c$.

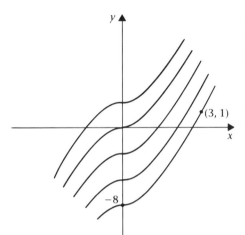

There is a family of solution curves which all satisfy the differential equation.

If, for example, you know that the graph passes through the point $(3, 1)$, then you can specify the particular solution as $y = \dfrac{1}{3}x^3 - 8$.

Where possible write down the equation of the particular solution curve which passes through the point $(0, 1)$ for each of the following differential equations.

(a) $\dfrac{dy}{dx} = 3x + 2$

(b) $\dfrac{dy}{dx} = 3x^2 - 2x - 1$

(c) $\dfrac{dy}{dx} = x \cos x$

(d) $\dfrac{dy}{dx} = x \cos x^2$

(e) $\dfrac{dy}{dx} = \cos x^2$

(f) $\dfrac{dy}{dx} = \dfrac{y + x}{y - x}$

Discuss why you are not able to solve all of the equations.

Differential equations frequently arise in mathematics and numerical methods are often the only way to solve them. While the rest of this chapter will concentrate on numerical methods, this section will give you some practice with differential equations which can be solved by 'simple' algebraic methods.

EXAMPLE 1

For the differential equation $\dfrac{dy}{dx} = 2x + \sin x$, find the value

of y when $x = 2$ for the particular solution through $(3, 4)$.

SOLUTION

$$y = \int (2x + \sin x)\,dx$$
$\Rightarrow\ y = x^2 - \cos x + c$, but $y = 4$ when $x = 3$
$\Rightarrow\ 4 = 3^2 - \cos 3 + c$
$\Rightarrow\ 4 = 9 + 0.99 + c$
$\Rightarrow\ c = -5.99$ (to 2 d.p.)
$\Rightarrow\ y = x^2 - \cos x - 5.99$ and so when $x = 2$, $y = -1.57$ (to 2 d.p.)

EXERCISE 2

1 Solve the following differential equations and in each case make a sketch showing some particular solutions.

(a) $\dfrac{dy}{dx} = e^x$ (b) $\dfrac{dy}{dx} = \cos 2x$ (c) $x^2 \dfrac{dy}{dx} + 1 = 0$

2 For each of the differential equations given below, find y when $x = 3$ for the particular solutions which pass through the point $(1, 0)$.

(a) $\dfrac{dy}{dx} = 4x^3$ (b) $\dfrac{dy}{dx} = 3x^2 - 2x + 2$

(c) $\dfrac{dy}{dx} = \dfrac{1}{x^3}$ (d) $\dfrac{dy}{dx} = 2e^{2x}$

3 A can of water is heated at a rate which decreases steadily with time. The temperature $y\,°C$ after t minutes satisfies the differential equation

$$\frac{dy}{dt} = 8 - \frac{4t}{3}$$

(a) Find y when $t = 4$ if $y = 32$ initially.

(b) Do you think the model will still be valid at time $t = 10$?

4E For each of the differential equations given below, find y when $x = 2$ for the particular solutions which pass through the origin.

(a) $\dfrac{dy}{dx} = \sin(3x + 2)$ (b) $\dfrac{dy}{dx} = x^2 e^{x^3}$ (c) $\dfrac{dy}{dx} = x \cos(x^2 + 1)$

5.3 Direction diagrams

From Newton's law of cooling, you know that the rate at which a cup of coffee cools is proportional to the number of degrees, y, that it is above room temperature.

The differential equation $\dfrac{dy}{dt} = -0.2y$ expresses this in symbols, for a particular cup for which the constant of proportionality is 0.2. The negative sign indicates that the coffee is cooling rather than heating up.

The equation $\dfrac{dy}{dt} = -0.2y$ also determines the shape of the (t, y) graph.

At any point, the gradient is -0.2 times the value of the y-coordinate of the point. For example, at any point with y-coordinate 40, the gradient is -8. This gives the direction of the graph at such points. You can show this with small line-segments of gradient -8.

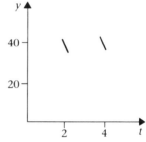

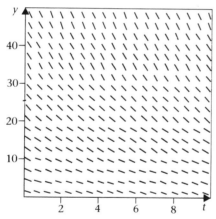

Similarly, you can calculate the direction at every point. This is shown in this **direction diagram** for some regularly spaced points in the first quadrant.

By looking at the direction diagram, it is clear that the graph is not a single curve but is a whole family of curves. There is a different cooling curve for each different starting temperature the cup could have.

The direction diagram can also be extended into the other three quadrants.

Complete the diagram for the second quadrant. What is represented by cooling curves in the second quadrant?

What would the third and fourth quadrants of this direction diagram represent? Complete these parts of the diagram.

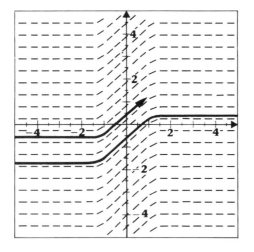

This is a direction diagram for the differential equation

$$\frac{dy}{dx} = \frac{1}{1 + x^4}$$

Each segment represents part of a solution through its centre. When sketching a solution curve it is important to try to imagine what the path of the solution might be as it follows its own path in the same general direction as the nearby line-segments. A curve which follows the direction of the line-segments is sketched on the direction diagram.

In the case above, the gradient is dependent only on x, so the line-segments in a vertical column (with fixed value of x) are all parallel.

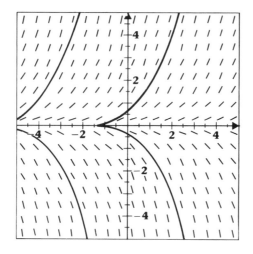

The family of solutions for

$$\frac{dy}{dx} = y$$

are parallel in a **horizontal** direction.

Tasksheet 2 is designed to give some insight into how the direction diagram is calculated and how it can be used for hand-sketching of solutions.

TASKSHEET 2 – *Direction diagrams (page 113)*

With a program such as the solution sketcher in *Real functions and graphs*, you can rapidly draw a short line-segment through any point and hence build up a solution to a differential equation by clicking together line-segments whose gradients are calculated by the computer to satisfy the differential equation.

You should have found that:

> (a) a differential equation has a family of solutions;
>
> (b) there is a single solution through each starting point, found by following the direction given by the differential equation.

EXERCISE 3

1   Use a solution sketcher with $-5 \leqslant x \leqslant 5$, $-4 \leqslant y \leqslant 4$ to display those solutions to the differential equation $\dfrac{dy}{dx} = -\dfrac{x}{2y}$ which pass through the following points:

(a) (0, 1)   (b) (0, 2)   (c) (0, 2.5)   (d) (0, 3)

Describe the family of curves.

2   Use a solution sketcher with $-4 \leqslant x \leqslant 4$, $0 \leqslant y \leqslant 6$ to display those solutions to the differential equation $\dfrac{dy}{dx} = -\dfrac{xy}{5}$ which pass through the following points:

(a) (0, 1)   (b) (0, 2)   (c) (0, 4)   (d) (0, 6)

Describe the family of curves.

3   Wilhelm's law states that, in a chemical reaction, the rate of change of mass is proportional to the mass of the reacting substance present at any instant. Explain briefly how this leads to the differential equation $\dfrac{dx}{dt} = -kx$, where k is a constant.

Consider the case $\dfrac{dx}{dt} = -0.5x$.

Use a solution sketcher with $0 \leqslant t \leqslant 5$, $0 \leqslant x \leqslant 10$ to display the solution which passes through the point (0, 8).

Explain the significance of the value 8, and investigate other curves in the family of solutions.

5.4 Numerical methods

Numerical methods for solving differential equations depend upon approximating the solution curve with a series of straight line-segments.

If (x, y) is a point on a graph, then the point $(x + dx, y + dy)$ is on the tangent. For a locally straight graph, and for small dx, the point $(x + dx, y + dy)$ is close to the graph.

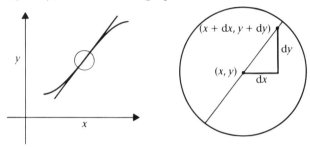

An approximate numerical solution can therefore be obtained by fixing a small numerical value for dx, then calculating a point further along the curve as $(x + dx, y + dy)$ and taking this as a new starting point. Consider a particular situation for the simple differential equation $\dfrac{dy}{dx} = 2x$ and starting from the point $(1, 4)$.

At $(1, 4)$ the gradient is 2, so a step along of $dx = 0.1$ will give a step up of $dy = 0.2$. The move along the tangent is from $(1, 4)$ to $(1.1, 4.2)$.

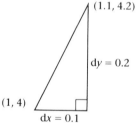

> What is the gradient at $(1.1, 4.2)$?
>
> Find the step up for a further step along of $dx = 0.1$. What point along the tangent at $(1.1, 4.2)$ is now reached?

Can you decide where you would be after three further steps of $dx = 0.1$, when $x = 1.5$? It may help to set the calculation out in a table, working down column by column:

	x	y	$\dfrac{dy}{dx}$	dx	dy	$x + dx$	$y + dy$
First step	1	4	2	0.1	0.2	1.1	4.2
Second step	1.1	4.2	2.2	0.1	0.22	1.2	4.42

In this example, the actual solution curve is $y = x^2 + 3$.

So $y = 4.21$ when $x = 1.1$, whereas $y = 4.2$ is obtained by moving along the tangent instead of the curve.

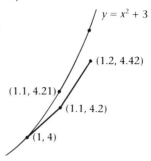

When $x = 1.5$, what value of y is found by moving along tangents with steps of d$x = 0.1$?

What is the value for y on the actual solution curve through $(1, 4)$? How could the accuracy of the step-by-step method have been improved, if necessary?

EXAMPLE 2

For the differential equation

$$\frac{dy}{dx} = \frac{y}{1 + x^4}$$

find the value of y when $x = 2$ for the particular solution through $(1, 6)$.

SOLUTION

The table below shows the start of the calculation, using five steps of d$x = 0.2$ and working to 3 significant figures.

x	y	$\dfrac{dy}{dx}$	dx	dy	$x + dx$	$y + dy$
1	6	3	0.2	0.6	1.2	6.6
1.2	6.6	2.15	0.2	0.43	1.4	7.03

Continue the calculations to obtain $y = 7.64$ when $x = 2$.

103

The step-by-step calculations are straightforward with a calculator but it is more efficient to use a program.

For the solution curve for $\dfrac{dy}{dx} = 2x$ which passes through (1, 4) you can use routines such as the following. The step size is H.

CASIO GRAPHICAL CALCULATOR

```
  1→X
  4→Y
0.1→H
Lbl 1
Y+2XH→Y
X+H→X
"X":X◢
"Y":Y◢
Goto 1
```

BBC BASIC

```
10 LET X=1
20 LET Y=4
30 LET H=0.1
40 LET Y=Y+2*X*H
50 LET X=X+H
60 PRINT X,Y
70 GOTO 40
```

EXERCISE 4

1 (a) What is the equation of the solution curve for $\dfrac{dy}{dx} = \cos x$ which passes through (0, 0)?

(b) Calculate the numerical solution of the differential equation $\dfrac{dy}{dx} = \cos x$ starting at $x = 0$, $y = 0$ with step 0.1. Record the values of x and y for $x = 0, 0.5, 1$, etc., giving y values to 1 decimal place. How accurate is the numerical solution for different values of x?

2 (a) What is the equation of the solution curve for $\dfrac{dy}{dx} = 4x^3$ which passes through (1, 0)? Find the value of y when $x = 2$.

(b) Use a numerical method, with a step size of 0.2, to find the value of y when $x = 2$.

3 (a) What is the equation of the solution curve for $\dfrac{dy}{dx} = \sin 2x$ which passes through (0, −0.5)?

(b) Using a step size of 0.1, find the percentage error in the numerical solution for y at $x = 1$.

4 (a) $\dfrac{dy}{dx} = 2x \;\Rightarrow\; y = x^2 + c$

For $\dfrac{dy}{dx} = 2x$, what is the particular solution curve through $(1, 2)$?

Plot this solution curve on graph paper for $-1 \leqslant x \leqslant 3$.

(b) Calculate a numerical solution of $\dfrac{dy}{dx} = 2x$ starting at $x = 1, y = 2$.

Using steps of size 0.2, record the values from $x = 1$ to 3 and round off the y values to 1 decimal place. Record also the values from $x = 1$ to -1. Plot the numerical solutions for $-1 \leqslant x \leqslant 3$ on the same diagram as your graph of the solution curve and comment on the accuracy of the numerical method.

(c) Repeat part (b) with step size 0.1. Comment on the improvement in accuracy obtained with the smaller step value.

5E For equations where you can find a solution curve by integration, it is possible to write a program to check the accuracy of the numerical method for different sized steps. The program could either print out both the numerical solution and the correct value of y as obtained by integration, or it could plot the numerical solutions and then superimpose the correct graph over them. Use one of these methods to investigate the accuracy of numerical solutions for $\dfrac{dy}{dx} = e^x$ for different step values, starting at $x = 0, y = 1$.

6E Write a table of values for a numerical solution to:

$$\frac{dy}{dx} = \frac{1}{1 + x^2}$$

starting at $x = 0, y = 0$, with step $dx = 0.1$, from $x = 0$ to $x = 4$. Record selected values of x and y sufficiently accurately to plot a graph.

Also write a table of selected values starting at $x = 0, y = 0$, with step $dx = -0.1$ and sketch the graph for the solution through $x = 0, y = 0$ from $x = -4$ to $+4$.

Does the graph have a shape you recognise? If not, reflect it in the line $y = x$ to consider x as a function of y. Suggest a possible relationship between x and y and check a few values to see if your graph is (approximately) in agreement with your suggestion.

Write a brief report on what you find.

5.5 Growth and decay

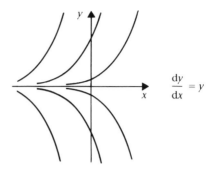

$$\frac{dy}{dx} = y$$

The differential equation $\dfrac{dy}{dx} = y$ generates a family of solution curves which look like the graphs of growth functions.

The equation $\dfrac{dy}{dx} = y$ cannot be solved by algebraic integration as it stands. However, a simple rearrangement is helpful:

$$\frac{dy}{dx} = y \;\Rightarrow\; \frac{dx}{dy} = \frac{1}{y}$$

$$\Rightarrow \qquad x = \int \frac{1}{y}\, dy$$

$$\Rightarrow \qquad x = \ln y + c$$

$$\Rightarrow \quad x + k = \ln y \qquad (k = -c)$$

$$\Rightarrow \qquad y = e^{x+k}$$

$$\Rightarrow \qquad y = e^{k}e^{x}$$

$$\Rightarrow \qquad y = Ae^{x} \qquad (A = e^{k})$$

The solution curves are indeed the graphs of growth functions.

> Check that you understand the analysis above. Generalise the argument to solve:
>
> $$\frac{dy}{dx} = \lambda y$$

Differential equations of the form $\dfrac{dy}{dx} = \lambda y$ generate families of solution curves which are the graphs of growth functions.

$$\frac{dy}{dx} = \lambda y \;\Rightarrow\; y = Ae^{\lambda x}$$

E X A M P L E   3

Earlier in the chapter, you considered the differential equation
$\dfrac{dx}{dt} = -0.5x$, where x kg was the mass of a reacting chemical
present t hours after the start of the reaction. Initially there was 8 kg
of the substance. Find the mass of the substance after 1 hour.

S O L U T I O N

$\dfrac{dx}{dt} = -0.5x \Rightarrow x = Ae^{-0.5t}$
When $t = 0, x = 8 \Rightarrow A = 8$
Then $x = 8e^{-0.5t}$ and, after 1 hour,
$\qquad x = 8e^{-0.5} \approx 4.85$
After 1 hour there is approximately 4.85 kg of the substance remaining.

E X A M P L E   4

A murder victim was discovered by the police at 6:00 a.m. The body
temperature of the victim was measured and found to be 25 °C. A
doctor arrived on the scene of the crime 30 minutes later and
measured the body temperature again. It was found to be 22 °C. The
temperature of the room had remained constant at 15 °C. The
doctor, knowing normal body temperature to be 37 °C, was able to
estimate the time of death of the victim. What would be your
estimate for the time of death?

S O L U T I O N

Assume Newton's law of cooling:

The rate of cooling at any instant is directly proportional to the
difference in temperature between the object and its surroundings.

t hours after 6 a.m., let the body temperature be y°C above the
temperature of the surroundings.

$\qquad \dfrac{dy}{dt} = \lambda y \Rightarrow y = Ae^{\lambda t}$

When $t = 0$ and $y = 10$,

$\qquad 10 = Ae^0 \Rightarrow A = 10$

When $t = 0.5$ and $y = 7$,

$\qquad 7 = 10e^{0.5\lambda} \Rightarrow 0.5\lambda = \ln 0.7$
$\qquad\qquad\qquad \Rightarrow \quad \lambda = -0.713 \text{ (to 3 s.f.)}$

So $y = 10e^{-0.713t}$

(a) Use the fact that death occurred when $y = 22$ to show that the doctor's estimate of the time of death would be 4:54 a.m.

(b) Compare this answer with that obtained earlier using numerical methods and comment on the discrepancy.

EXERCISE 5

1 Find the equation of the solution curve of

$$\frac{dy}{dx} = -y$$

which passes through the point (0, 2).

2 The mass, x kg, of a substance satisfies the differential equation

$$\frac{dx}{dt} = -0.1x$$

where t is the time in hours after the start of a chemical reaction.

(a) Initially there was 2 kg of the substance. Find a formula for x in terms of t.

(b) Hence calculate the time taken for the mass of the substance to be halved.

3 Boiling water is left in a room and cools to 90°C in 5 minutes. If the room temperature is 20°C, how long will the water take to cool to 60°C?

4 A colony of insects has a population of 100 and is growing at the rate of 50 insects per day. If the rate of growth at any time is proportional to the population size at that time, how many insects will there be after 10 days?

5 A radioactive substance decays at a rate proportional to its mass. When the mass of a sample of the substance is 0.020 g it is decaying at a rate of 0.001 g per day. There are m grams left after t days.

(a) Formulate a differential equation connecting m and t.

(b) How long does the sample take to decay to 0.010 g?

 TASKSHEET 3E — Carbon dating (page 115)

5.6 Formulating differential equations

In this chapter you have studied both numerical and analytical methods for solving differential equations. The geometrical picture of the family of solution curves is also valuable. In particular, it indicates the effect of different initial conditions.

The relative advantages and disadvantages of solving a differential equation by inspection or by a step-by-step method can be summarised as follows:

> Solving a differential equation by inspection has the advantage that precise solutions are obtained.
>
> The power of a step-by-step method is that it can be applied to calculate a solution however complicated the gradient function may be.

To be able to apply either of these methods you must be able to formulate the differential equation correctly. This section considers a few examples of formulation.

EXAMPLE 5

High on the moors, perched on a rocky crag, lies a most curious boulder. It has fascinated the locals and tourists alike for years, for it is almost perfectly spherical in shape. Over the years it has gradually been eroded by the action of the winds, but it has retained its basic shape. In fact, according to the locals, it now has half the diameter it had 100 years ago. 'Be gone in another 100 years' they say. Are they right?

SOLUTION

Set up a model	The locals will be right only if there is a linear relationship between the radius of the boulder and time. To decide if this is the case you need to make some assumptions about the rate of erosion and decide upon the variables and units to be used.

Volume of boulder $V\,\text{cm}^3$
Radius of boulder $r\,\text{cm}$
Time from 100 years ago t years

It is reasonable to assume that the rate of erosion is proportional to the surface area, $A = 4\pi r^2$. Since the rate of erosion is $-\dfrac{dV}{dt}$, the important differential equation is

$$-\frac{dV}{dt} = kA \qquad \text{i.e.} \quad \frac{dV}{dt} = -4k\pi r^2$$

Analyse the problem	Since $V = \dfrac{4}{3}\pi r^3$,

$$\frac{dV}{dt} = \frac{4}{3}\pi \times 3r^2 \frac{dr}{dt}, \text{ by the chain rule}$$

$$= 4\pi r^2 \frac{dr}{dt}$$

So $4\pi r^2 \dfrac{dr}{dt} = -4k\pi r^2$

$$\Rightarrow \quad \frac{dr}{dt} = -k$$

Interpret /validate	The radius decreases at a constant rate and so the boulder **will** be gone in another 100 years. You cannot validate this conclusion directly although you could find out known facts about erosion rates. In fact, it is unlikely that the boulder will retain its shape as it is eroded.

EXERCISE 6

1 The volume of a large spherical snowball decreases as it melts at a rate proportional to its surface area at any instant.

(a) Express this statement in symbols.

(b) Given that a snowball of radius 30 cm takes 10 days to melt, find an expression for the radius r in terms of the time t.

(c) After how many days will

(i) the radius be halved;   (ii) the volume be halved?

2   In a lake, about 2000 newly hatched fish survive each year. However, about 10% of the fish in the lake die each year as the result of disease, predators or old age. These observations lead to the hypothesis that:

$$\frac{dy}{dt} = \alpha + \beta y, \text{ where } y \text{ is the number of fish present}$$

(a) Explain why $\beta = -0.1$ and state the value of α.

(b) In what units are y and $\frac{dy}{dt}$ measured?

(c) The lake had a stable population of 20000 fish before a careless discharge of chemicals killed 5000 fish. Estimate how long it will take for the population to reach 19000.

(d) Write down the differential equation which will apply if 12% of the fish die each year and 2500 newly hatched fish survive.

3E   A full tea urn contains a hundred cupfuls.

Nine cups are filled from the urn in the first minute. The rate of flow is believed to be proportional to the square root of the height of the liquid in the urn.

Explain the relationship in symbols, stating their units and meaning.

How long does it take to fill four dozen cups?

[This question can be tackled either analytically or numerically. Use whichever method you prefer.]

After working through this chapter, you should:

1   be able to interpret and formulate differential equations;

2   know how to find the differential equation associated with a given family of curves;

3   be able to draw and interpret direction diagrams;

4   be able to calculate approximate solutions by a step-by-step method;

5   know how to obtain solutions by inspection when appropriate;

6   have developed an appreciation of the mathematical modelling implicit in the formulation and solution of differential equations;

7   have a deeper understanding of rates of change;

8   be able to use appropriate software.

Cooling curves

> You will need: Datasheet 2 – Cooling curves
> SMP gradient measurer

Newton's law of cooling can be verified by experiment.

1 Some coffee was made and its temperature was monitored continually as it was allowed to cool down over a 2-hour period.

Graph 1 shows a plot of the temperature difference between the coffee and the room, $y°C$, and the time in minutes.

(a) Use the gradient measurer to find the gradient of the cooling curve at 10, 30, 50, 70 and 90 minutes.

(b) Plot the gradient from (a) against the temperature difference at the time.

(c) What sort of relationship appears to exist between the gradient and the temperature difference?

(d) Explain in physical terms what the gradient represents.

(e) Express the gradient using calculus notation.

(f) Express the relationship found in (c) in a fully symbolised form.

2 Firm conclusions should not be drawn on the basis of single experiment.

Graph 2 shows three cooling curves, each for a different cup of coffee.

(a) Explain why the three cups of coffee can have different temperatures at the time $t = 0$.

(b) Using the gradient measurer, measure the gradient of each curve at the temperature difference $y = 40°C$. Comment on your result.

(c) Pick another temperature difference and find the gradient on each curve for this value of y.

(d) Make a general statement regarding what appears to be true from (b) and (c).

(e) All three curves represent the cooling of cups of coffee. In particular, one of these curves is for the cup of coffee from question 1. Which one?

(f) Write down an equation, with the gradient represented as a derivative, that can represent any one, or all, of these cooling curves.

Direction diagrams

1 Use a solution sketcher to draw a direction diagram for a cup of coffee cooling according to the equation $\dfrac{\mathrm{d}y}{\mathrm{d}t} = -0.2\,y$. 'Click together' direction segments to obtain suitable cooling curves to estimate how long it would take the cup to cool,

(a) from $y = 80$ to $y = 40$;

(b) from $y = 40$ to $y = 20$.

2 Using either an appropriate computer program, or (with a little patience) sketch by hand, a direction diagram for

$$\frac{\mathrm{d}y}{\mathrm{d}x} = x$$

(Use ranges $x = -5$ to 5, $y = -5$ to 5.) Sketch a solution through (0, 1).

3 Sketch the direction diagram for $\dfrac{\mathrm{d}y}{\mathrm{d}x} = -y$. What happens to solutions which start with y **negative** as x increases?

4 One of the following pictures is the direction diagram for $\dfrac{\mathrm{d}y}{\mathrm{d}x} = x - y$; the other is the direction diagram for $\dfrac{\mathrm{d}y}{\mathrm{d}x} = x + y$. Which is which? In the case of $\dfrac{\mathrm{d}y}{\mathrm{d}x} = x - y$, sketch a few solution curves and suggest what happens to y as x increases.

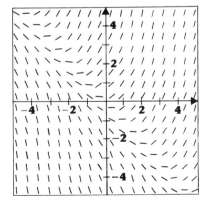 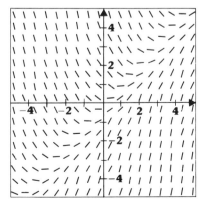

5   A murder victim was discovered by the police at 6:00 a.m. The body temperature of the victim was measured and found to be 25°C. A doctor arrived on the scene of the crime 30 minutes later and measured the body temperature again. It was found to be 22°C. The temperature of the room had remained constant at 15°C. The doctor, knowing normal body temperature to be 37°C, was able to estimate the time of death of the victim.

Find the rate of cooling over this half hour in degrees per hour. Estimate the time of death if this rate had remained constant.

Explain why $\dfrac{dy}{dt} = -0.6y$ is a better model and draw a direction diagram by hand or with an appropriate program. Sketch the cooling curve through the point (0, 10) and use it to get a better estimate for the time of death. Improve your estimate by using a program to 'click together' the appropriate direction segments.

6E   (This is an extension exercise for individuals or the whole class.)

Use a solution sketcher to investigate various differential equations, such as:

$$\frac{dy}{dx} = xy, \qquad \frac{dy}{dx} = e^x, \qquad \frac{dy}{dx} = \sin x, \qquad \frac{dy}{dx} = y \sin x, \qquad \frac{dy}{dx} = \sqrt{x},$$

$$\frac{dy}{dx} = x^2 + y^2$$

or others of your own choice. Write up what you find. In particular:

- Do the differential equations always have many solutions?

- Is there always a single solution through a given point?

- Can you say when two solutions differ by a constant?

- Do you notice anything else of interest?

Carbon dating

Radioactive chemical elements

The isotopes (see below) of many of the chemical elements are radioactive. This means that the structures of their atoms are unstable and the atoms readily decay to form other stable elements, releasing radiation in the process. There are three main types of radiation: alpha particles, which are essentially helium nuclei; beta particles, which are very fast moving electrons; and gamma rays, which are electromagnetic radiation of very high intensity.

For example, uranium-238 is radioactive and decays to eventually become lead-207. (238 and 207 are the atomic weights of uranium and lead respectively.)

Half-life

The half-life of a radioactive isotope is the time it takes for half the radioactive atoms in a sample to decay. In other words, if a sample of radioactive substance contains N atoms at some particular time, then the time it takes for this to decay so that $\frac{N}{2}$ atoms remain is the half-life.

Isotopes

Isotopes are different atoms of the same element, in that the nuclei of the atoms are different. All nuclei of a certain element contain the same number of protons, thus defining the atomic number and the characteristic chemical properties, but isotopes contain different numbers of neutrons in the nuclei.

Half-lives vary from a fraction of a second to millions of years. Some examples are:

uranium-238	4.5×10^9 years	iodine-128	25 minutes
carbon-14	5730 years	lawrencium-257	8 seconds
radium-226	1600 years	polonium-214	1.64×10^{-4} seconds

Representation as a differential equation

The principles of radioactivity were discovered and developed at the beginning of the twentieth century by the New Zealand physicist Ernest Rutherford (1871–1937) while he was at McGill University in Canada. It was for his work in this field that he was awarded the Nobel Prize for chemistry in 1908.

Rutherford discovered that if at a particular time, t, a sample of radioactive substance contains N atoms of the radioactive element per unit mass of the substance, then the number of atoms decreases with time according to the differential equation:

$$\frac{dN}{dt} = -kN$$

Radio carbon dating

One of the applications of this differential equation and its solution is found in archaeology. In a scientific paper published in 1949, the American chemist Professor Willard F. Libby first proposed a figure for the half-life of the radioactive isotope of carbon, carbon-14. He showed, further, how it could be used to date wooden artefacts and other remains containing carbon found on archaeological sites. This was a breakthrough of great significance for archaeology and, in 1961, Libby received the Nobel Prize for his work.

Libby first calculated the half-life of carbon-14 as 5568 years, but the accepted value is now about 5730 years. This is equivalent to about 1% of the carbon-14 atoms decaying every 83 years. Carbon-14 emits beta particles, becoming nitrogen in the process.

Carbon has three isotopes. Carbon-12 accounts for roughly 99% of carbon in the world and carbon-13 the other 1%. So the occurrence of carbon-14 is tiny, the ratio of carbon-14 to carbon-12 atoms being about $1 : 10^{12}$. It is the fact that it is possible to measure the radioactivity of carbon-14 that makes it possible to date ancient remains, whether they are of wood, flesh or bone. Carbon-14 in living organisms is radioactive, and its radioactivity level is measured at 6.68 pico-curies per gram (1 pico-curie is equivalent to 3.7×10^{10} disintegrations per second), but the loss is made up by natural processes and there is only a net decay after the carbon-containing organism dies.

Carbon dating is usually accepted as a dating method valid up to about 40000 years, when carbon-14 levels become too low to measure. Some error is inevitable, not least because radiation itself is a random process. Great care must be taken to avoid contamination of artefacts with fresh carbon when preparing to measure their radioactivity, otherwise gross errors could occur. However, the carbon dating method has been verified back to about 5000 BC using dendrochronology. Dendrochronology is the counting of tree rings, one new ring being formed in the trunk for each year of growth. This check is possible since some trees are incredibly old and yet still growing. For instance, the bristle-cone pines of California are over 4000 years old and still growing.

Solution of the differential equation

$$\frac{dN}{dt} = -kN \implies N = N_0 e^{-kt}$$

where N_0 is the number of atoms of carbon-14 per unit mass in the substance at time $t = 0$.

1 Show that if the half-life of carbon-14 is 5730 years then

$$k \approx \frac{1}{8300}$$

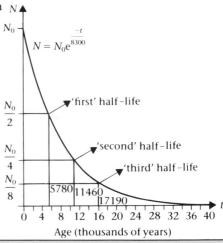

Age (thousands of years)

If you know how many carbon-14 atoms there are per gram for a dead organism (for example, a piece of wood) then knowing how many there should have been when the organism was alive (i.e. a tree) would enable you to estimate the time that has elapsed since its death. It would be difficult to establish the number of carbon-14 atoms in one gram of substance. What can be measured with accuracy is the radioactivity level of any carbon-14 atoms present in a gram of substance.

Suppose $R(t)$ represents the measured radioactivity of carbon-14 at time t. Because radioactivity is proportional to the total number of carbon-14 atoms present it follows that

$$\frac{R(0)}{R(t)} = \frac{N_0 e^0}{N_0 e^{\frac{-t}{8300}}}$$

2   Explain how this equation can be rearranged to give

$$t = 8300 \ln \left(\frac{R(0)}{R(t)} \right)$$

How old is Pete Marsh?

Pete Marsh is a name popularly given to the remains of a man whose body was found in a bog in Lindow Moss in Cheshire. The man had apparently been murdered by garroting before being thrown in the bog; but when did it happen? Readings of the carbon-14 radioactivity levels from the body were about 5.3 pico-curies per gram.

It is reasonable to assume that his radioactivity would have been 6.68 when he was alive and so the time that has elapsed since the death of Pete Marsh can be estimated by

$$t = 8300 \ln \left(\frac{6.68}{5.3} \right) = 1920 \text{ years.}$$

This suggests that the murder took place nearly 2000 years before the body was discovered. Latest estimates from the Radiocarbon Unit at Oxford University suggest that Pete Marsh died between 2 BC and AD 119, at the time of the Roman occupation of Britain.

3   Historical records indicate that the Egyptian king, Sneferu, died some time between 2700 BC and 2550 BC. Radioactivity levels from carbon-containing artefacts in his tomb gave a reading of about 3.8 pico-curies per gram.

   Does this reading agree with the historical records?

4   For a long time, historians believed that the origins of agriculture were in the Near East around 4500 BC. Archaeological investigations at the ancient city of Jericho (in modern day Israel) found farming implements that gave a radiocarbon reading of 2.8 pico-curies per gram.

   Why did this lead to a storm in historical circles?

Solutions

1 The power of Pythagoras

1.1 Pythagoras and right-angled triangles

EXERCISE 1

1 Calling the hypotenuse x,

(a) $x^2 = 10^2 + 24^2 = 676 \Rightarrow x = 26\,\text{cm}$
[This is simply a scaled up 5, 12, 13 triangle.]

(b) $x^2 = 4.9^2 + 16.8^2 = 306.25 \Rightarrow x = 17.5\,\text{cm}$

2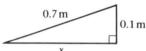

From the diagram
$WT^2 = 3.7^2 + 0.9^2$
$\Rightarrow WT = 3.8\,\text{km}$

So Westminster Abbey and the Tower of London are 3.8 km apart.

3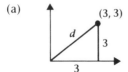

$x^2 = 0.7^2 - 0.1^2$
$\Rightarrow x = 0.69\,\text{m}$

The space needed in front of the step is 69 cm, virtually the full length of the plank!

1.2 The equation of a circle

(a) Use Pythagoras' theorem to find the distance of the point (3, 3) from the origin.

(b) Use Pythagoras' theorem to find the distance of the point (4, 6) from the point (1, 2).

(a)

$d^2 = 3^2 + 3^2 = 18$
so $d = \sqrt{18} \approx 4.24$

(b)

$d^2 = 3^2 + 4^2 = 25$
so $d = 5$
(or, since the triangle is clearly a
3, 4, 5 triangle, $d = 5$)

EXERCISE 2

1 Using the formula $x^2 + y^2 = r^2$ the equations are:

(a) $x^2 + y^2 = 225$

(b) $x^2 + y^2 = 16$

(c) $x^2 + y^2 = 2.53$ since $2\pi r = 10$, so $r = 1.59$

(d) $x^2 + y^2 = 400$ since the radius is the distance of (12, 16) from the
origin

2 Using the formula $(x - a)^2 + (y - b)^2 = r^2$, the equations are:

(a) $(x - 1)^2 + (y - 1)^2 = 9$ (b) $(x + 4)^2 + (y - 6)^2 = 64$

3

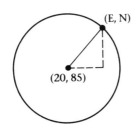

By Pythagoras,
$(E - 20)^2 + (N - 85)^2 = 18^2$

The equation fails to take account of varying
levels of visibility.

4 If (x, y, z) are the coordinates of a point on the sphere, the (distance)^2 of this
point from the centre (2, 3, 1) is:

$$(x - 2)^2 + (y - 3)^2 + (z - 1)^2$$

The equation of the sphere is therefore:

$$(x - 2)^2 + (y - 3)^2 + (z - 1)^2 = 4^2 = 16$$

5 (a) The square of the distance from (3, 2) to (1, 4) is:

$$(3 - 1)^2 + (2 - 4)^2 = 8$$

Since $8 < 9$, the (radius)^2, it follows that (3, 2) lies inside the circle.

A similar argument works for (b), (c), (d).

(b) outside   (c) the point lies on the sphere   (d) inside

119

6E The distance between the centres is:

$$\sqrt{[(120-160)^2+(150-180)^2+(30-40)^2]}$$
$$=\sqrt{2600}\approx 51$$

Since this is greater than the sum of
the two radii, they do not intersect.

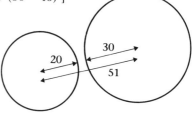

7E Suppose the equation is $(x-a)^2+(y-b)^2=r^2$.
Each point which lies on this circle will satisfy the equation.

$$(6-a)^2+(9-b)^2=r^2$$
$$(13-a)^2+(-8-b)^2=r^2$$
$$(-4-a)^2+(-15-b)^2=r^2$$

These simplify to

$$a^2+b^2-12a-18b+117=r^2 \qquad ①$$
$$a^2+b^2-26a+16b+233=r^2 \qquad ②$$
$$a^2+b^2+8a+30b+241=r^2 \qquad ③$$

Eliminating r^2,

$① - ② \Rightarrow 14a-34b-116=0$
$③ - ② \Rightarrow 34a+14b+8=0$

giving $a=1$, $b=-3$, $r=13$
So the centre is $(1,-3)$, radius 13 and equation $(x-1)^2+(y+3)^2=169$.

8E Suppose the equation is $(x-a)^2+(y-b)^2=100$.
Since it passes through $(10, 9)$ and $(8, -5)$ it follows that

$$(10-a)^2+(9-b)^2=100$$
$$(8-a)^2+(-5-b)^2=100$$

which become $a^2+b^2-20a-18b+81=0 \qquad ①$
and $a^2+b^2-16a+10b-11=0 \qquad ②$

Firstly, eliminate a^2+b^2 by subtracting ① from ②

$$4a+28b=92$$
i.e. $a=23-7b$

Now substitute for a in ① to obtain a quadratic in b

$$(23-7b)^2+b^2-20(23-7b)-18b+81=0$$

which reduces to $b^2-4b+3=0$
Hence $b=1$ or $b=3$
If $b=1$, $a=16$, and if $b=3$, $a=2$

So the two equations are

$$(x-16)^2+(y-1)^2=100$$
and $(x-2)^2+(y-3)^2=100$

$(-6,-3)$ lies on the second circle.

1.3 Trigonometric identities

> Sketch the graphs of $y = 2\sin^2 x$ and $y = 3\cos x$ to verify that these are sensible solutions.

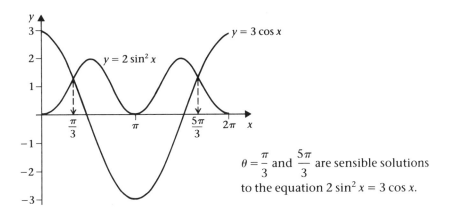

$\theta = \dfrac{\pi}{3}$ and $\dfrac{5\pi}{3}$ are sensible solutions to the equation $2\sin^2 x = 3\cos x$.

EXERCISE 3

1 (a) $1 + \cos x = 3(1 - \cos^2 x) \implies 3\cos^2 x + \cos x - 2 = 0$

   (b) $(3c - 2)(c + 1)$

   (c) $48.2°, \quad 180°, \quad 311.8°$

2 (a) $\tan\theta = \frac{2}{3} \qquad \theta = 33.7°, 213.7°$

   (b) $\tan\theta = 1.6 \qquad \theta = 58.0°, 238.0°$

   (c) $\tan 2\theta = 1.4 \qquad \theta = 27.2°, 117.2°, 207.2°, 297.2°$

3 (a) $0, \quad \dfrac{2\pi}{3}, \quad \dfrac{4\pi}{3}, \quad 2\pi$

   (b) $\dfrac{\pi}{3}, \quad \dfrac{4\pi}{3}$

   (c) $1.05\left(=\dfrac{\pi}{3}\right), \quad 1.82, \quad 4.46, \quad 5.24\left(=\dfrac{5\pi}{3}\right)$

4E (a) Let N be the foot of the perpendicular from C to OP.
Then $PC^2 = NC^2 + PN^2$, where $NC = 100\sin\theta$ and
$PN = 130 - 100\cos\theta$.

   (b) $PC^2 = 100^2 \sin^2\theta + 100^2 \cos^2\theta - 2 \times 130 \times 100\cos\theta + 130^2$
$= 26\,900 - 26\,000\cos\theta$

   (c) $-32.2° \leqslant \theta \leqslant 32.2°$

1.4 $r \sin(\theta + \alpha)$

1 (a) $3 \sin \theta + 2 \cos \theta = r \sin(\theta + \alpha)$
where $r = \sqrt{(3^2 + 2^2)} = 3.61$
and $\tan \alpha = \frac{2}{3} \Rightarrow \alpha = 33.7°$

(b) $3.61 \sin(\theta + 33.7°) = 3$
$\Rightarrow \theta + 33.7° = 56.3°$ or $123.7°$
$\Rightarrow \qquad \theta = 22.6°$ or $90°$

2 (a) $5 \sin \theta + 12 \cos \theta$ is equivalent to $r \sin(\theta + \alpha)$ where r and α can be found from the triangle below.

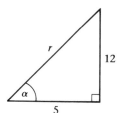

$r = 13, \quad \tan \alpha = \frac{12}{5}$
giving $\alpha = 67.4°$

Since $5 \sin \theta + 12 \cos \theta = 13 \sin(\theta + 67.4°)$, the maximum value is 13, which occurs when $\theta + 67.4° = 90°$, i.e. at $\theta = 22.6°$.

(b)

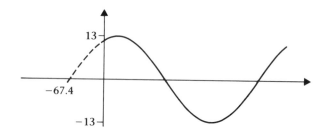

$13 \sin(\theta + 67.4°) = 9$
$\Rightarrow \qquad \theta + 67.4° = 43.8°, \quad 136.2°, \quad 403.8°,$ etc.
$\Rightarrow \qquad \theta = 68.8°$ or $336.4°$

3 (a) (i) $AD = 2 \times 3 \sin \theta = 6 \sin \theta$

(ii) $AB = 2 \times 4 \cos \theta = 8 \cos \theta$

(iii) perimeter $= 12 \sin \theta + 16 \cos \theta$

(b) $12 \sin \theta + 16 \cos \theta = 14$
$\Rightarrow 3 \sin \theta + 4 \cos \theta = 3.5$

(c) $3 \sin \theta + 4 \cos \theta = 5 \sin(\theta + 53.1°)$
$\Rightarrow \theta = 82°$
The sides have length 5.9 and 1.1.

(d) The largest perimeter is 20, which occurs when $\theta = 36.9°$.

4E (a) B will move in a circle because OB remains constant.
The radius OB $= \sqrt{(6^2 + 3^2)} = \sqrt{45} = 6.71\,\text{m}$

(b)

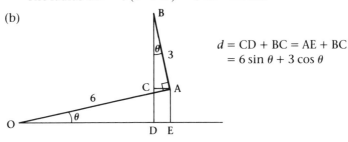

$d = \text{CD} + \text{BC} = \text{AE} + \text{BC}$
$= 6 \sin \theta + 3 \cos \theta$

(c)

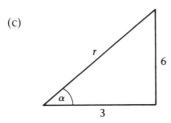

$6 \sin \theta + 3 \cos \theta = r \sin(\theta + \alpha)$
where $r = \sqrt{(6^2 + 3^2)} = 6.71\,\text{m}$
$\tan \alpha = \frac{3}{6} = \frac{1}{2} \Rightarrow \alpha = 26.6°$

(d) The maximum distance is $6.71\,\text{m}$, when $\sin(\theta + 26.6°) = 1$,
i.e. $\theta = 63.4°$.

1.5 Addition formulas

EXERCISE 5

1 (a) $\sin(x + 60°) = \sin x \cos 60° + \cos x \sin 60°$
$$= \frac{1}{2} \sin x + \frac{\sqrt{3}}{2} \cos x$$

(b) –

2 (a) $\sin(x + \pi) = \sin x \cos \pi + \cos x \sin \pi$
$$= -\sin x$$

(b)

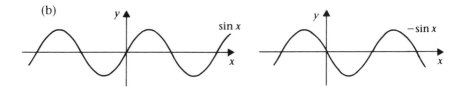

A translation of the sine graph by $-\pi$ in the x-direction has the same effect as a reflection in the x-axis.

3 (a) $\cos(A + B) + \cos(A - B) = \cos A \cos B - \sin A \sin B$
$$+ \cos A \cos B + \sin A \sin B$$
$$= 2 \cos A \cos B$$

(b) $\cos(A - B) - \cos(A + B) = 2 \sin A \sin B$

4 (a) $\sin(45° + 30°) = \sin 45° \cos 30° + \cos 45° \sin 30°$

$$= \frac{1}{\sqrt{2}} \times \frac{\sqrt{3}}{2} + \frac{1}{\sqrt{2}} \times \frac{1}{2}$$

$$= \frac{\sqrt{3} + 1}{2\sqrt{2}}$$

  (b) $\sin 15° = \sin(45° - 30°) = \dfrac{\sqrt{3} - 1}{2\sqrt{2}}$

5 $\dfrac{63}{65}$

6E $\tan\left(x + \dfrac{\pi}{4}\right) = \dfrac{\sin\left(x + \dfrac{\pi}{4}\right)}{\cos\left(x + \dfrac{\pi}{4}\right)} = \dfrac{\dfrac{1}{\sqrt{2}}(\cos x + \sin x)}{\dfrac{1}{\sqrt{2}}(\cos x - \sin x)}$

$$= \frac{\cos x + \sin x}{\cos x - \sin x}$$

Dividing the numerator and the denominator by $\cos x$,

$$\tan\left(x + \frac{\pi}{4}\right) = \frac{1 + \tan x}{1 - \tan x}$$

7E (a) $\sin 3x = \sin 2x \cos x + \cos 2x \sin x$
$$= (2 \sin x \cos x) \cos x + (1 - 2 \sin^2 x) \sin x$$
$$= 2 \sin x (1 - \sin^2 x) + \sin x - 2 \sin^3 x$$
$$= 3 \sin x - 4 \sin^3 x$$

  (b) $\cos 3x = 4 \cos^3 x - 3 \cos x$

1.6 Solution of non-right-angled triangles: the cosine rule

EXERCISE 6

1 5.76 cm

2 (a) $\cos A = \dfrac{b^2 + c^2 - a^2}{2bc}$

  (b) 34.0°, 44.4°, 101.5°

3 (a) $a^2 = 10^2 + 7^2 - 2 \times 10 \times 7 \cos 45°$ $a = 7.1$ cm

  (b) $a^2 = 10^2 + 7^2 - 2 \times 10 \times 7 \cos 120°$ $a = 14.8$ cm

  (c) $a = 17$ cm

4

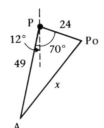

If at the time of the collision the *Poisson* was x km from the *Archimedes*, x can be found using the cosine rule.

$$x^2 = 49^2 + 24^2 - 2 \times 49 \times 24 \cos 82°$$
$$= 2649$$
So $x = 51.5$ km

It seems likely that *Archimedes* was out of radio range.

It does seem surprising that a trawler is only carrying a radio with maximum range 50 km, that the signal was not received in Plymouth and that, in the Channel, no other vessels were closer.

1.7   Solution of non-right-angled triangles: the sine rule

> What is the height of the cliff?

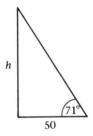

$$\frac{h}{50} = \tan 71°$$
$$\Rightarrow h = 50 \tan 71° = 145 \text{ m}$$

E X E R C I S E   7

1 (a) $\dfrac{8}{\sin 80°} = \dfrac{5}{\sin \theta} \Rightarrow \sin \theta = \dfrac{5 \sin 80°}{8} = 0.6155$, giving $\theta = 38°$

Thus the third angle is $62°$ and $\dfrac{8}{\sin 80°} = \dfrac{x}{\sin 62°}$

giving $x = \dfrac{8 \sin 62°}{\sin 80°} = 7.17$ cm

(b) $\theta = 27.4°$, the third angle is $22.6°$ and $x = 10.05$ mm

2 (a) $x^2 = 18^2 + 10^2 - 2 \times 18 \times 10 \cos 35°$
$\Rightarrow x = 11.4$ cm
$\dfrac{\sin \theta}{10} = \dfrac{\sin 35°}{11.4} \Rightarrow \theta = 30.2°$
The remaining angles are $30.2°$ and $114.8°$

(b) $x = 100.3$ m
The remaining angles are $49.3°$ and $58.7°$.

3 (a) 51.6 cm^2 (b) 3420 m^2 (to 3 s.f.)

4 (a) Using the cosine rule, $x = 43.2\,\text{m}$.
Using the sine rule, the remaining angles are $33.2°$ and $46.8°$.

(b) Using Pythagoras, the remaining side is $24\,\text{mm}$
[$(7, 24, 25)$ is a Pythagorean triple].

Using the properties of sin and cos, the angles are $16.3°$ and $73.7°$.

(c) Using the sine rule, the second angle is $41.9°$.
Using the angle sum of a triangle, the third angle is $73.1°$.
Using the sine rule, the remaining side is $40.1\,\text{cm}$.

(d) The angles are $48.2°$, $58.4°$ and $73.4°$.

2 Vector geometry

2.1 Vectors and position vectors

EXERCISE 1

1

(a) The direction vector is $\begin{bmatrix} 7 \\ 7 \end{bmatrix} - \begin{bmatrix} 4 \\ 1 \end{bmatrix} = \begin{bmatrix} 3 \\ 6 \end{bmatrix}$, so the line is $\begin{bmatrix} x \\ y \end{bmatrix} = \begin{bmatrix} 4 \\ 1 \end{bmatrix} + t\begin{bmatrix} 3 \\ 6 \end{bmatrix}$

(b) $\begin{bmatrix} x \\ y \end{bmatrix} = \begin{bmatrix} 2 \\ 1 \end{bmatrix} + t\begin{bmatrix} -3 \\ 4 \end{bmatrix}$

(c) $\begin{bmatrix} x \\ y \end{bmatrix} = \begin{bmatrix} 5 \\ 1 \end{bmatrix} + t\begin{bmatrix} -2 \\ 4 \end{bmatrix}$

(d) The direction vector is $\begin{bmatrix} 1 \\ 1 \end{bmatrix}$ and the line passes through $\begin{bmatrix} 0 \\ 0 \end{bmatrix}$.

$\begin{bmatrix} x \\ y \end{bmatrix} = t\begin{bmatrix} 1 \\ 1 \end{bmatrix}$

(e) $\begin{bmatrix} x \\ y \end{bmatrix} = t\begin{bmatrix} 0 \\ 1 \end{bmatrix}$

2 (a) $\overrightarrow{PQ} = \mathbf{q} - \mathbf{p} = \begin{bmatrix} 5 \\ -2 \end{bmatrix} - \begin{bmatrix} 3 \\ 1 \end{bmatrix} = \begin{bmatrix} 2 \\ -3 \end{bmatrix}$

$\overrightarrow{SR} = \mathbf{r} - \mathbf{s} = \begin{bmatrix} 2 \\ -4 \end{bmatrix} - \begin{bmatrix} 0 \\ -1 \end{bmatrix} = \begin{bmatrix} 2 \\ -3 \end{bmatrix}$

Since $\overrightarrow{PQ} = \overrightarrow{SR}$ the vectors are of the same length and direction, i.e. PQ is parallel to SR and equal in length, so PQRS is a parallelogram.

(b) It follows that $\overrightarrow{PS}$ must also equal $\overrightarrow{QR}$.

3 (a) (i) $\overrightarrow{OD} = \begin{bmatrix} 6 \\ 0 \\ 10 \end{bmatrix}$ $\overrightarrow{OE} = \begin{bmatrix} 0 \\ 8 \\ 10 \end{bmatrix}$

(ii) $\overrightarrow{AB} = \mathbf{b} - \mathbf{a} = \begin{bmatrix} -6 \\ 8 \\ 0 \end{bmatrix}$ $\overrightarrow{AD} = \begin{bmatrix} 0 \\ 0 \\ 10 \end{bmatrix}$ $\overrightarrow{AC} = \begin{bmatrix} -6 \\ 0 \\ 10 \end{bmatrix}$

$\overrightarrow{AE} = \begin{bmatrix} -6 \\ 8 \\ 10 \end{bmatrix}$ $\overrightarrow{DE} = \begin{bmatrix} -6 \\ 8 \\ 0 \end{bmatrix}$

(b) (i) $\overrightarrow{OM} = \overrightarrow{OA} + \tfrac{1}{2}\overrightarrow{AB} = \begin{bmatrix} 3 \\ 4 \\ 0 \end{bmatrix}$ $\overrightarrow{ON} = \overrightarrow{OD} + \tfrac{1}{2}\overrightarrow{DE} = \begin{bmatrix} 3 \\ 4 \\ 10 \end{bmatrix}$

(ii) $\overrightarrow{AN} = \overrightarrow{ON} - \overrightarrow{OA} = \begin{bmatrix} -3 \\ 4 \\ 10 \end{bmatrix}$ $\overrightarrow{ME} = \overrightarrow{OE} - \overrightarrow{OM} = \begin{bmatrix} -3 \\ 4 \\ 10 \end{bmatrix}$

(iii) $\overrightarrow{AN} = \overrightarrow{ME}$, which is to be expected since AN is parallel to ME and of equal length.

4 (a) $\mathbf{a} = \begin{bmatrix} 8 \\ 0 \\ 0 \end{bmatrix}$ $\mathbf{b} = \begin{bmatrix} 8 \\ 10 \\ 0 \end{bmatrix}$ $\mathbf{c} = \begin{bmatrix} 0 \\ 10 \\ 0 \end{bmatrix}$ $\mathbf{d} = \begin{bmatrix} 4 \\ 2 \\ 3 \end{bmatrix}$ $\mathbf{e} = \begin{bmatrix} 4 \\ 8 \\ 3 \end{bmatrix}$

NB. You can find **d** and **e** by viewing the roof from above:

(b) $\overrightarrow{AD} = \mathbf{d} - \mathbf{a} = \begin{bmatrix} -4 \\ 2 \\ 3 \end{bmatrix}$ $\overrightarrow{OD} = \begin{bmatrix} 4 \\ 2 \\ 3 \end{bmatrix}$ $\overrightarrow{BE} = \begin{bmatrix} -4 \\ -2 \\ 3 \end{bmatrix}$ $\overrightarrow{CE} = \begin{bmatrix} 4 \\ -2 \\ 3 \end{bmatrix}$

(c) By Pythagoras, the length of $\overrightarrow{AD}$ is $\sqrt{(4^2 + 2^2 + 3^2)} = \sqrt{29} = 5.4\,\text{m}$

2.2 Equations of lines

Why is it necessary to have **different** parameters, λ and μ, for the two lines?

If λ were used for the second line as well as the first it would not be possible to generate points independently.

> (a) Will lines in three dimensions always meet?
>
> (b) What will happen if the method of example 2 is applied in three dimensions?

(a) No. See the diagram.

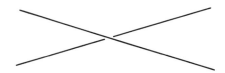

(b) The x and y coordinates can still be equated to find λ and μ. Then, when these values of λ and μ are substituted into the z coordinates, two possibilities exist:

  (i) the coordinates are equal and so the lines meet;

  (ii) the coordinates are unequal and so the lines do not meet.

E X E R C I S E   2

1 $\begin{bmatrix} x \\ y \end{bmatrix} = \begin{bmatrix} 3 \\ 0 \end{bmatrix} + \lambda \begin{bmatrix} -3 \\ 3 \end{bmatrix}$ and $\begin{bmatrix} x \\ y \end{bmatrix} = \begin{bmatrix} 1 \\ 0 \end{bmatrix} + \mu \begin{bmatrix} 2 \\ 2 \end{bmatrix}$

$\Rightarrow 3 - 3\lambda = 1 + 2\mu$

and $3\lambda = 2\mu$ giving $\lambda = \dfrac{1}{3}$ $\mu = \dfrac{1}{2}$

and a point of intersection $\begin{bmatrix} 2 \\ 1 \end{bmatrix}$

2   (a) OG

(b) $\lambda = 0$ gives $\begin{bmatrix} 4 \\ 0 \\ 3 \end{bmatrix}$; $\lambda = 1$ gives $\begin{bmatrix} 0 \\ 5 \\ 3 \end{bmatrix}$ i.e. EG

(c) CE   (d) BD

3   Writing $\mathbf{r}$ for $\begin{bmatrix} x \\ y \\ z \end{bmatrix}$ gives

(a) $\mathbf{r} = \overrightarrow{OA} + \lambda \overrightarrow{AB} = \begin{bmatrix} 4 \\ 0 \\ 0 \end{bmatrix} + \lambda \begin{bmatrix} 0 \\ 5 \\ 0 \end{bmatrix}$

(b) $\mathbf{r} = \overrightarrow{OA} + \lambda\,\overrightarrow{AC} = \begin{bmatrix} 4 \\ 0 \\ 0 \end{bmatrix} + \lambda \begin{bmatrix} -4 \\ 5 \\ 0 \end{bmatrix}$

(c) $\mathbf{r} = \overrightarrow{OA} + \lambda\,\overrightarrow{AF} = \begin{bmatrix} 4 \\ 0 \\ 0 \end{bmatrix} + \lambda \begin{bmatrix} 0 \\ 5 \\ 3 \end{bmatrix}$

(d) $\mathbf{r} = \overrightarrow{OA} + \lambda\,\overrightarrow{AG} = \begin{bmatrix} 4 \\ 0 \\ 0 \end{bmatrix} + \lambda \begin{bmatrix} -4 \\ 5 \\ 3 \end{bmatrix}$.

4 When the y components are equal $\quad 3 - \lambda = -3 + \mu$
and when the z components are equal $\quad \lambda = \mu$

i.e. $\lambda = \mu = 3$

$\lambda = 3 \Rightarrow x = 4 - 3 = 1 \qquad \mu = 3 \Rightarrow x = 4 - 3 = 1$

Hence the vertex is at $\begin{bmatrix} 1 \\ 0 \\ 3 \end{bmatrix}$.

2.3 Scalar products

How would the scalar product of the following pairs of vectors be related?

(i) (ii) 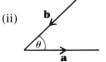 (iii)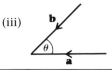

In (i) $\mathbf{a} \cdot \mathbf{b} = |a|\,|b| \cos\theta$

In (ii) $\mathbf{b}$ is in the opposite direction so $\mathbf{a} \cdot \mathbf{b}$ is $|a|\,|b| \cos(180 - \theta) = -|a|\,|b| \cos\theta$

In (iii) both $\mathbf{a}$ and $\mathbf{b}$ are pointing towards the origin so $\mathbf{a} \cdot \mathbf{b} = |a|\,|b| \cos\theta$.

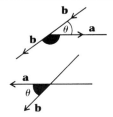

How can the scalar product be generalised to vectors in three dimensions?

If the two vectors are $\mathbf{a} = \begin{bmatrix} a_1 \\ a_2 \\ a_3 \end{bmatrix}$ and $\mathbf{b} = \begin{bmatrix} b_1 \\ b_2 \\ b_3 \end{bmatrix}$ the definition extends

naturally to $a_1 b_1 + a_2 b_2 + a_3 b_3$ or $ab \cos\theta$, where, in order to find a, the length of $\mathbf{a}$, it is now necessary to use the three-dimensional form of Pythagoras' theorem.

EXERCISE 3

1 (a) Using $\cos \theta = \dfrac{\mathbf{a} \cdot \mathbf{b}}{ab}$ gives $\cos \theta = \dfrac{\begin{bmatrix} 5 \\ 2 \end{bmatrix} \cdot \begin{bmatrix} 3 \\ 2 \end{bmatrix}}{\sqrt{(25 + 4)}\sqrt{(9 + 4)}} = \dfrac{5 \times 3 + 2 \times 2}{\sqrt{29}\sqrt{13}} = \dfrac{19}{\sqrt{377}}$

$\Rightarrow \theta = 11.9°$

(b) $\cos \theta = \dfrac{\begin{bmatrix} 5 \\ 2 \end{bmatrix} \cdot \begin{bmatrix} -3 \\ 2 \end{bmatrix}}{\sqrt{(25 + 4)}\sqrt{(9 + 4)}} = \dfrac{-15 + 4}{\sqrt{29}\sqrt{13}} = \dfrac{-11}{\sqrt{377}}$

$\Rightarrow \theta = 124.5°$

2

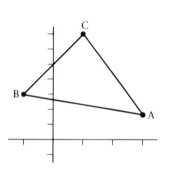

(a) $\overrightarrow{AB} = \mathbf{b} - \mathbf{a} = \begin{bmatrix} -1 \\ 3 \end{bmatrix} - \begin{bmatrix} 3 \\ 2 \end{bmatrix} = \begin{bmatrix} -4 \\ 1 \end{bmatrix}$

$\overrightarrow{AC} = \mathbf{c} - \mathbf{a} = \begin{bmatrix} 1 \\ 7 \end{bmatrix} - \begin{bmatrix} 3 \\ 2 \end{bmatrix} = \begin{bmatrix} -2 \\ 5 \end{bmatrix}$

(b) Both vectors must be pointing away from A.

$\cos A = \dfrac{\overrightarrow{AB} \cdot \overrightarrow{AC}}{|AB|\,|AC|} = \dfrac{8 + 5}{\sqrt{17}\,\sqrt{29}} = \dfrac{13}{\sqrt{493}}$

$\Rightarrow A = 54.2°$

3 If θ is the required angle

(a) $\cos \theta = \dfrac{12 \times 8 + 1 \times 4 + (-12) \times 1}{\sqrt{(12^2 + 1^2 + (-12)^2)}\,\sqrt{(8^2 + 4^2 + 1^2)}} = \dfrac{88}{\sqrt{289}\,\sqrt{81}} = \dfrac{88}{153} = 0.575$

$\theta = 54.9°$

(b) $\cos \theta = \dfrac{4 \times 7 + (-1) \times 4 + (-8)(-4)}{\sqrt{(16 + 1 + 64)}\,\sqrt{(49 + 16 + 16)}} = \dfrac{56}{\sqrt{81}\,\sqrt{81}} = \dfrac{56}{81} = 0.691$

$\theta = 46.3°$

4 $\overrightarrow{PQ} = \begin{bmatrix} -7 \\ 4 \\ 4 \end{bmatrix} \quad \overrightarrow{PR} = \begin{bmatrix} 4 \\ 8 \\ -1 \end{bmatrix}$

$\Rightarrow \cos P = \dfrac{-28 + 32 - 4}{\sqrt{(49 + 16 + 16)}\,\sqrt{(16 + 64 + 1)}} = 0 \Rightarrow P = 90°$

$\overrightarrow{QP} = -\overrightarrow{PQ} = \begin{bmatrix} 7 \\ -4 \\ -4 \end{bmatrix} \quad \overrightarrow{QR} = \begin{bmatrix} 11 \\ 4 \\ -5 \end{bmatrix}$

$\Rightarrow \cos Q = \dfrac{77 - 16 + 20}{\sqrt{(49 + 16 + 16)}\,\sqrt{(121 + 16 + 25)}} = \dfrac{81}{9\sqrt{162}} = \dfrac{9}{\sqrt{2}\,\sqrt{81}} = \dfrac{1}{\sqrt{2}}$

$\Rightarrow Q = 45° \quad$ and $\quad R = 180° - 90° - 45° = 45°$

5 $\overrightarrow{AB} = \begin{bmatrix} 1 \\ 6 \\ -5 \end{bmatrix}$ $\overrightarrow{DC} = \begin{bmatrix} 1 \\ 6 \\ -5 \end{bmatrix}$

Since $\overrightarrow{AB} = \overrightarrow{DC}$, AB is parallel to DC and of equal length. Hence ABCD is a parallelogram.

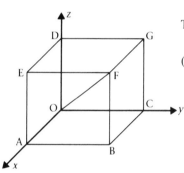 $\overrightarrow{AD} = \begin{bmatrix} 4 \\ 1 \\ 2 \end{bmatrix}$

$|AB| = \sqrt{(1 + 36 + 25)} = \sqrt{62} = 7.87$
$|AD| = \sqrt{(16 + 1 + 4)} = \sqrt{21} = 4.58$

$\cos A = \dfrac{\overrightarrow{AB} \cdot \overrightarrow{AD}}{|AB||AD|} = \dfrac{4 + 6 - 10}{\sqrt{62}\,\sqrt{21}} = 0$

$\Rightarrow A = 90°$ and the parallelogram is a rectangle.

6E Consider a unit cube as shown.

The longest diagonal is $\overrightarrow{OF} = \begin{bmatrix} 1 \\ 1 \\ 1 \end{bmatrix}$.

(a) You require DOF

$\cos\ DOF = \dfrac{\overrightarrow{OD} \cdot \overrightarrow{OF}}{|OD||OF|} = \dfrac{\begin{bmatrix} 0 \\ 0 \\ 1 \end{bmatrix} \cdot \begin{bmatrix} 1 \\ 1 \\ 1 \end{bmatrix}}{1 \times \sqrt{3}} = \dfrac{1}{\sqrt{3}}$

$\Rightarrow$ angle DOF = 54.7°

(b) One face diagonal is OE

$\Rightarrow \cos\ EOF = \dfrac{\overrightarrow{OE} \cdot \overrightarrow{OF}}{|OE||OF|} = \dfrac{\begin{bmatrix} 1 \\ 0 \\ 1 \end{bmatrix} \cdot \begin{bmatrix} 1 \\ 1 \\ 1 \end{bmatrix}}{\sqrt{2}\sqrt{3}} = \dfrac{2}{\sqrt{6}}$

$\Rightarrow$ angle EOF = 35.3°

(c) One other longest diagonal is CE, represented by $\begin{bmatrix} 1 \\ 0 \\ 1 \end{bmatrix} - \begin{bmatrix} 0 \\ 1 \\ 0 \end{bmatrix} = \begin{bmatrix} 1 \\ -1 \\ 1 \end{bmatrix}$

If the angle between the diagonals is θ,

$\cos\ \theta = \dfrac{\overrightarrow{CE} \cdot \overrightarrow{OF}}{|CE||OF|} = \dfrac{\begin{bmatrix} 1 \\ -1 \\ 1 \end{bmatrix} \cdot \begin{bmatrix} 1 \\ 1 \\ 1 \end{bmatrix}}{\sqrt{3}\sqrt{3}} = \dfrac{1}{3}$

$\Rightarrow \theta = 70.5°$

131

2.4 Properties of the scalar product

EXERCISE 4

1   (a) $|a| = \sqrt{(3^2 + 2^2)} = \sqrt{13}$ $|b| = \sqrt{(5^2 + 3^2)} = \sqrt{34}$
        $|c| = \sqrt{[(-2)^2 + 3^2]} = \sqrt{13}$

    (b)   **a . b** $= 3 \times 5 + 2 \times 3 = 21$ **b . c** $= 5 \times (-2) + 3 \times 3 = -1$
        c . a $= (-2) \times 3 + 3 \times 2 = 0$

    (c)   **c** is perpendicular to **a**.

    (d)   By inspection $\begin{bmatrix} 3 \\ -5 \end{bmatrix}$ is perpendicular to $\begin{bmatrix} 5 \\ 3 \end{bmatrix}$ $\left(\text{or any multiple of} \begin{bmatrix} 3 \\ -5 \end{bmatrix}\right)$.

2   (a)   **a . b** $= 2 + 0 - 2 = 0$ **b . c** $= 4 + 0 - 4 = 0$
        c . a $= 8 - 10 + 2 = 0$

    (b)   All three sets of vectors are mutually perpendicular.

3   (a) $\mathbf{c} = \begin{bmatrix} 2 \\ 4 \end{bmatrix}$ (b) $\mathbf{d} = \mathbf{a} - \mathbf{b} = \begin{bmatrix} 16 \\ -8 \end{bmatrix}$ (c)   **c . d** $= 32 - 32 = 0$

    (d)

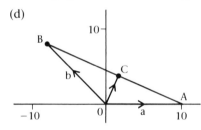

Since **c . d** $= 0$,   **c** is perpendicular to **d**.
i.e. OC is perpendicular to AB.

OC is called an **altitude** of the triangle.

4E   (a) $\mathbf{b} - \mathbf{h}$ is the vector $\overrightarrow{HB}$ and since $\overrightarrow{HB}$ is perpendicular to $\overrightarrow{OA}$,
        a . (b − h) $= 0$

    (b) $\overrightarrow{HA}$ is perpendicular to $\overrightarrow{OB}$ so **b . (a − h)** $= 0$

    (c)   **b . (a − h) − a . (b − h)** $= 0$
        $\Rightarrow$ **b . a − b . h − a . b + a . h** $= 0$
        $\Rightarrow$ **a . h − b . h** $= 0$ (since **b . a = a . b**)
        $\Rightarrow$ **(a − b) . h** $= 0$

    (d) $\mathbf{a} - \mathbf{b}$ is the vector $\overrightarrow{BA}$ and this is perpendicular to $\overrightarrow{OH}$.
        Thus $\overrightarrow{OH}$ is also an altitude of the triangle.
        i.e. in any triangle, the three altitudes are concurrent. (They intersect in
        a single point.)

5E   (a) $\overrightarrow{OR} = \overrightarrow{OP} + \overrightarrow{PR} = \overrightarrow{OP} + \overrightarrow{OQ} = \mathbf{p} + \mathbf{q}$
        $\overrightarrow{QP} = \mathbf{p} - \mathbf{q}$

    (b)   Using the result that **a . (b + c) = a . b + a . c**,
        (p + q) . (p − q) = p . p − p . q + q . p − q . q
          $= p^2 - \mathbf{p . q} + \mathbf{q . p} - q^2$ (since **p . p** $= p^2$
                                            and **p . q = q . p**)

(c) (i) $\overrightarrow{OR} \cdot \overrightarrow{OP} = 0 \Rightarrow \overrightarrow{OR}$ is perpendicular to $\overrightarrow{QP}$.

     (ii) If $\overrightarrow{OR} \cdot \overrightarrow{OP} = 0$

         then $(\mathbf{p} + \mathbf{q}) \cdot (\mathbf{p} - \mathbf{q}) = 0$

         i.e. $p^2 - q^2 = 0$

    $\Rightarrow \mathbf{p} = \mathbf{q}$ and the parallelogram is a rhombus.

This proves the well-known result that the diagonals of a rhombus intersect at right angles.

2.5 Vector equations of planes

EXERCISE 5

1 Taking A as a particular point on the plane

$$\overrightarrow{AB} = \begin{bmatrix} -3 \\ -1 \\ 1 \end{bmatrix} \quad \overrightarrow{AC} = \begin{bmatrix} -6 \\ -2 \\ 4 \end{bmatrix}$$

$$\begin{bmatrix} x \\ y \\ z \end{bmatrix} = \begin{bmatrix} 2 \\ 3 \\ 1 \end{bmatrix} + \lambda \begin{bmatrix} -3 \\ -1 \\ 3 \end{bmatrix} + \mu \begin{bmatrix} -6 \\ -2 \\ 4 \end{bmatrix}$$

2 The three points at which the plane cuts the axes are

$$A \begin{bmatrix} 2 \\ 0 \\ 0 \end{bmatrix}, \quad B \begin{bmatrix} 0 \\ -1 \\ 0 \end{bmatrix} \quad \text{and} \quad C \begin{bmatrix} 0 \\ 0 \\ 3 \end{bmatrix}$$

$$\overrightarrow{AB} = \begin{bmatrix} -2 \\ -1 \\ 0 \end{bmatrix} \quad \overrightarrow{AC} = \begin{bmatrix} -2 \\ 0 \\ 3 \end{bmatrix} \quad \text{so} \quad \begin{bmatrix} x \\ y \\ z \end{bmatrix} = \begin{bmatrix} 2 \\ 0 \\ 0 \end{bmatrix} + \lambda \begin{bmatrix} -2 \\ -1 \\ 0 \end{bmatrix} + \mu \begin{bmatrix} -2 \\ 0 \\ 3 \end{bmatrix}$$

3 (a) $\overrightarrow{OD} = \begin{bmatrix} -2 \\ 2 \\ 3 \end{bmatrix}$

    (b) Taking O as the particular point on OAD, $\begin{bmatrix} x \\ y \\ z \end{bmatrix} = \lambda \begin{bmatrix} -2 \\ 2 \\ 3 \end{bmatrix} + \mu \begin{bmatrix} 0 \\ 4 \\ 0 \end{bmatrix}$

$$\overrightarrow{DC} = \begin{bmatrix} -2 \\ -2 \\ -3 \end{bmatrix} \quad \overrightarrow{DB} = \begin{bmatrix} -2 \\ 2 \\ -3 \end{bmatrix}, \quad \begin{bmatrix} x \\ y \\ z \end{bmatrix} = \begin{bmatrix} -2 \\ 2 \\ 3 \end{bmatrix} + \lambda \begin{bmatrix} -2 \\ -2 \\ -3 \end{bmatrix} + \mu \begin{bmatrix} -2 \\ 2 \\ -3 \end{bmatrix} \quad \text{for BCD.}$$

4 $\overrightarrow{AB} = \begin{bmatrix} -3 \\ -1 \\ 3 \end{bmatrix} \quad \overrightarrow{AC} = \begin{bmatrix} -6 \\ -2 \\ 6 \end{bmatrix}$

i.e. $\overrightarrow{AC} = 2\overrightarrow{AB}$ and the three points are collinear.

2.6   Cartesian equation of a plane

> (a) What are the difficulties involved in talking about the **gradient** of a plane?
>
> (b) How does the idea of a **normal vector** help in fixing the orientation of a plane in space?

(a) Since a plane is two-dimensional it is not possible to choose a single direction in which to measure the gradient.

(b) Since the plane has a unique direction to which it is perpendicular, it is possible to specify its orientation using that vector, the normal vector.

> (a) Why are $\mathbf{n} \cdot \mathbf{b}$ and $\mathbf{n} \cdot \mathbf{c}$ zero?
>
> (b) Why is $\mathbf{n} \cdot \mathbf{a}$ a constant?
>
> (c) How does this relate to the Cartesian equation of the plane in the form $ax + by + cz = d$?

(a) Since $\mathbf{n} \perp \mathbf{b}$ and $\mathbf{n} \perp \mathbf{c}$, $\mathbf{n} \cdot \mathbf{b} = \mathbf{n} \cdot \mathbf{c} = 0$

(b) $\mathbf{n} \cdot \mathbf{a}$ is constant because $\mathbf{a}$ is a fixed vector in the plane and so $\mathbf{n} \cdot \mathbf{a}$ is the product of two fixed vectors.

(c) The equation thus reduces to $\mathbf{n} \cdot \mathbf{r} = \mathbf{n} \cdot \mathbf{a}$ or $\mathbf{n} \cdot \mathbf{r} = d$, where d is a constant.

In the case of $ax + by + cz = d$, $\mathbf{n} = \begin{bmatrix} a \\ b \\ c \end{bmatrix}$, $\mathbf{r} = \begin{bmatrix} x \\ y \\ z \end{bmatrix}$.

EXERCISE 6

1 (a) $\mathbf{n} \cdot \mathbf{r} = \mathbf{n} \cdot \mathbf{a} \Rightarrow \begin{bmatrix} 2 \\ -3 \\ 1 \end{bmatrix} \cdot \begin{bmatrix} x \\ y \\ z \end{bmatrix} = \begin{bmatrix} 2 \\ -3 \\ 1 \end{bmatrix} \cdot \begin{bmatrix} 0 \\ 0 \\ 0 \end{bmatrix}$

i.e. $2x - 3y + z = 0$

(b) $\begin{bmatrix} 2 \\ -3 \\ 1 \end{bmatrix} \cdot \begin{bmatrix} x \\ y \\ z \end{bmatrix} = \begin{bmatrix} 2 \\ -3 \\ 1 \end{bmatrix} \cdot \begin{bmatrix} 3 \\ 1 \\ -2 \end{bmatrix}$ gives $2x - 3y + z = 1$

(c) $\begin{bmatrix} 5 \\ -2 \\ 0 \end{bmatrix} \cdot \begin{bmatrix} x \\ y \\ z \end{bmatrix} = \begin{bmatrix} 5 \\ -2 \\ 0 \end{bmatrix} \cdot \begin{bmatrix} 3 \\ 1 \\ -2 \end{bmatrix} \Rightarrow 5x - 2y = 13$

2 (a) $\mathbf{n} = \begin{bmatrix} 1 \\ 1 \\ 0 \end{bmatrix}$, $\quad \begin{bmatrix} 1 \\ 1 \\ 0 \end{bmatrix} \cdot \begin{bmatrix} x \\ y \\ z \end{bmatrix} = \begin{bmatrix} 1 \\ 1 \\ 0 \end{bmatrix} \cdot \begin{bmatrix} 1 \\ 0 \\ 0 \end{bmatrix}$ $\quad$ i.e. $x + y = 1$

(b) $\mathbf{n} = \begin{bmatrix} -1 \\ 1 \\ 0 \end{bmatrix}$, $\quad \begin{bmatrix} -1 \\ 1 \\ 0 \end{bmatrix} \cdot \begin{bmatrix} x \\ y \\ z \end{bmatrix} = \begin{bmatrix} -1 \\ 1 \\ 0 \end{bmatrix} \cdot \begin{bmatrix} 0 \\ 0 \\ 0 \end{bmatrix}$ $\quad$ i.e. $-x + y = 0$ or $y = x$

Although this looks like the equation of a line, it represents a plane, formed by the lines $y = x$ corresponding to various values of z.

(c) $\mathbf{n} = \begin{bmatrix} 1 \\ 1 \\ 1 \end{bmatrix}$, $\quad \begin{bmatrix} 1 \\ 1 \\ 1 \end{bmatrix} \cdot \begin{bmatrix} x \\ y \\ z \end{bmatrix} = \begin{bmatrix} 1 \\ 1 \\ 1 \end{bmatrix} \cdot \begin{bmatrix} 1 \\ 0 \\ 0 \end{bmatrix}$ $\quad$ i.e. $x + y + z = 1$

(d) $\mathbf{n} = \begin{bmatrix} 1 \\ 1 \\ 1 \end{bmatrix}$, $\quad \begin{bmatrix} 1 \\ 1 \\ 1 \end{bmatrix} \cdot \begin{bmatrix} x \\ y \\ z \end{bmatrix} = \begin{bmatrix} 1 \\ 1 \\ 1 \end{bmatrix} \cdot \begin{bmatrix} 1 \\ 1 \\ 0 \end{bmatrix}$ $\quad$ i.e. $x + y + z = 2$

(e) $\mathbf{n} = \begin{bmatrix} 0 \\ 0 \\ 1 \end{bmatrix}$, $\quad \begin{bmatrix} 0 \\ 0 \\ 1 \end{bmatrix} \cdot \begin{bmatrix} x \\ y \\ z \end{bmatrix} = \begin{bmatrix} 0 \\ 0 \\ 1 \end{bmatrix} \cdot \begin{bmatrix} 0 \\ 0 \\ 0 \end{bmatrix}$ $\quad$ i.e. $z = 0$

3 (a) $\mathbf{c} = \begin{bmatrix} 0 \\ 0 \\ 4 \end{bmatrix}$ $\quad$ (b) $\overrightarrow{CA} = \begin{bmatrix} 2 \\ 0 \\ -4 \end{bmatrix}$ $\quad \overrightarrow{CB} = \begin{bmatrix} 0 \\ 3 \\ -4 \end{bmatrix}$

(c) $\mathbf{r} = \begin{bmatrix} 0 \\ 0 \\ 4 \end{bmatrix} + \lambda \begin{bmatrix} 2 \\ 0 \\ -4 \end{bmatrix} + \mu \begin{bmatrix} 0 \\ 3 \\ -4 \end{bmatrix}$

(d) $x = 2\lambda$ $\qquad$ ①
$\quad\;\; y = 3\mu$ $\qquad$ ②
$\quad\;\; z = 4 - 4\lambda - 4\mu$ $\quad$ ③

(e) ① $\Rightarrow \lambda = \frac{1}{2}x$ $\quad$ ② $\Rightarrow \mu = \frac{1}{3}y$
$\quad$ So ③ $\Rightarrow z = 4 - 2x - \frac{4}{3}y$
$\quad$ i.e. $6x + 4y + 3z = 12$

(f) $\mathbf{n} = \begin{bmatrix} 6 \\ 4 \\ 3 \end{bmatrix}$

4E The coordinates of the vertices are A $(1, 0, 0)$ $\quad$ B $(0, 1, 0)$ $\quad$ C $(-1, 0, 0)$
$\quad$ D $(0, -1, 0)$ $\quad$ E $(0, 0, 1)$ $\quad$ F $(0, 0, -1)$

(a) The vector equation of AEB is:

$$\begin{bmatrix} x \\ y \\ z \end{bmatrix} = \begin{bmatrix} 1 \\ 0 \\ 0 \end{bmatrix} + \lambda \begin{bmatrix} -1 \\ 0 \\ 1 \end{bmatrix} + \mu \begin{bmatrix} -1 \\ 1 \\ 0 \end{bmatrix}$$

giving the Cartesian equation $x + y + z = 1$

The vector equation of DCF is

$$\begin{bmatrix} x \\ y \\ z \end{bmatrix} = \begin{bmatrix} 0 \\ -1 \\ 0 \end{bmatrix} + \lambda \begin{bmatrix} -1 \\ 1 \\ 0 \end{bmatrix} + \mu \begin{bmatrix} 0 \\ 1 \\ -1 \end{bmatrix}$$

giving $x + y + z = -1$

[Or both planes may be found by inspection.]

(b) Since both have normal vector $\begin{bmatrix} 1 \\ 1 \\ 1 \end{bmatrix}$ the planes are parallel.

(c) ECB is $x - y - z = -1$
and FAD is $x - y - z = 1$

2.7 Finding angles

EXERCISE 7

1 (a) $\mathbf{n}_1 = \begin{bmatrix} 1 \\ 1 \\ 1 \end{bmatrix}$ $\mathbf{n}_2 = \begin{bmatrix} 2 \\ 3 \\ 1 \end{bmatrix}$ $\cos \theta = \dfrac{2 + 3 + 1}{\sqrt{3}\ \sqrt{14}} = \dfrac{6}{\sqrt{42}}$

$\Rightarrow \theta = 22.2°$

(b) $\mathbf{n}_1 = \begin{bmatrix} 1 \\ -3 \\ -2 \end{bmatrix}$ $\mathbf{n}_2 = \begin{bmatrix} 5 \\ 0 \\ 2 \end{bmatrix}$ $\cos \theta = \dfrac{5 - 4}{\sqrt{14}\ \sqrt{29}} = \dfrac{1}{\sqrt{406}}$

$\Rightarrow \theta = 87.2°$

(c) $\mathbf{n}_1 = \begin{bmatrix} 1 \\ 0 \\ -2 \end{bmatrix}$ $\mathbf{n}_2 = \begin{bmatrix} 0 \\ 1 \\ 3 \end{bmatrix}$ $\cos \theta = \dfrac{-6}{\sqrt{5}\ \sqrt{10}} = \dfrac{-6}{\sqrt{50}}$

$\Rightarrow \theta = 148.1°$ or, taking the acute angle, $31.9°$

2 (a) The direction vectors for the two lines are $\begin{bmatrix} 2 \\ 1 \end{bmatrix}$ and $\begin{bmatrix} -1 \\ 1 \end{bmatrix}$.

The angle between them is given by $\cos \theta = \dfrac{-2 + 1}{\sqrt{5}\ \sqrt{2}} = \dfrac{-1}{\sqrt{10}}$

$\Rightarrow \theta = 108.4°$ or $71.6°$

(b) Taking direction vectors $\begin{bmatrix} -1 \\ 0 \\ 3 \end{bmatrix}$ and $\begin{bmatrix} -2 \\ 3 \\ 4 \end{bmatrix}$ gives

$\cos \theta = \dfrac{2 + 12}{\sqrt{10}\ \sqrt{29}} = \dfrac{14}{\sqrt{290}}$

$\Rightarrow \theta = 34.7°$

3 $\mathbf{n} = \begin{bmatrix} 2 \\ 3 \\ -1 \end{bmatrix}$ so $\cos\theta = \dfrac{\begin{bmatrix} 2 \\ 1 \\ 1 \end{bmatrix}\begin{bmatrix} 2 \\ 3 \\ -1 \end{bmatrix}}{\sqrt{6}\,\sqrt{14}} = \dfrac{6}{\sqrt{84}} \Rightarrow \theta = 49.1°$

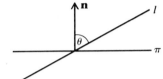

The required angle between the normal and the plane is:

$$90° - 49.1° = 40.9°$$

4 $\mathbf{n} = \begin{bmatrix} 1 \\ 1 \\ 1 \end{bmatrix}$ $\quad \mathbf{n}_1 = \begin{bmatrix} -1 \\ 1 \\ 1 \end{bmatrix}$ $\quad \cos\theta = \dfrac{-1 + 1 + 1}{\sqrt{3}\,\sqrt{3}} = \dfrac{1}{3} \Rightarrow \theta = 70.5°$

Since this is a 'typical' regular octahedron the dihedral angle is $70.5°$.

5E (a)

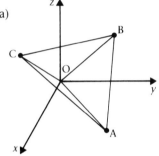

(b) $OA = \sqrt{(1^2 + 1^2 + 0^2)} = \sqrt{2} \qquad OB = \sqrt{(0^2 + 1^2 + 1^2)} = \sqrt{2}$
$OC = \sqrt{(1^2 + 0^2 + 1^2)} = \sqrt{2}$

$$\overrightarrow{AB} = \begin{bmatrix} -1 \\ 0 \\ 1 \end{bmatrix} \Rightarrow |AB| = \sqrt{(1^2 + 0^2 + 1^2)} = \sqrt{2}$$

$$\overrightarrow{AC} = \begin{bmatrix} 0 \\ -1 \\ 1 \end{bmatrix} \Rightarrow |AC| = \sqrt{(0^2 + 1^2 + 1^2)} = \sqrt{2}$$

$$\overrightarrow{BC} = \begin{bmatrix} 1 \\ -1 \\ 0 \end{bmatrix} \Rightarrow |BC| = \sqrt{(1^2 + 1^2 + 0^2)} = \sqrt{2}$$

(c) OAB is $x - y + z = 0$ with normal $\begin{bmatrix} 1 \\ -1 \\ 1 \end{bmatrix}$

OAC is $x - y - z = 0$ with normal $\begin{bmatrix} 1 \\ -1 \\ -1 \end{bmatrix}$

$$\cos\theta = \dfrac{1 + 1 - 1}{\sqrt{3}\,\sqrt{3}} = \dfrac{1}{3} \Rightarrow \theta = 70.5°,\text{ which is the dihedral angle of the tetrahedron.}$$

137

(d) BC is $\mathbf{r} = \begin{bmatrix} 0 \\ 1 \\ 1 \end{bmatrix} + \lambda \begin{bmatrix} 1 \\ -1 \\ 0 \end{bmatrix}$ direction $\begin{bmatrix} 1 \\ -1 \\ 0 \end{bmatrix}$

OA is $\mathbf{r} = \mu \begin{bmatrix} 1 \\ 1 \\ 0 \end{bmatrix}$

$$\cos \theta = \frac{1 - 1 + 0}{\sqrt{2} \, \sqrt{2}} = 0 \implies \theta = 90°$$

i.e. opposite pairs of edges of a regular tetrahedron are perpendicular.

(e) The direction of BC is $\begin{bmatrix} 1 \\ -1 \\ 0 \end{bmatrix}$.

The normal to OAC is $\begin{bmatrix} 1 \\ -1 \\ -1 \end{bmatrix}$.

$$\implies \cos \theta = \frac{1 + 1}{\sqrt{2} \, \sqrt{3}} = \frac{2}{\sqrt{6}} \qquad \theta = 35.3°$$

Thus the angle between the edge and
the face is $90° - 35.3° = 54.7°$.
Hence the height h of the tetrahedron is
BC $\sin 54.7° = \sqrt{2} \sin 54.7° \approx 1.15$.

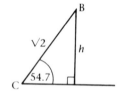

3 Binomials

3.1 Binomial expansions

> Use the method of multiplying brackets shown below to explain why
> Pascal's triangle generates the coefficients of powers of $a + b$.

The coefficients of a particular power of $a + b$ are formed by adding pairs of
coefficients of the previous power, just as in Pascal's triangle:

1   3   3   1
    └─┬─┘
      ↓
      6

EXERCISE 1

1 (a) $(a + b)^6 = a^6 + 6a^5b + 15a^4b^2 + 20a^3b^3 + 15a^2b^4 + 6ab^5 + b^6$

(b) $(p - q)^5 = p^5 - 5p^4q + 10p^3q^2 - 10p^2q^3 + 5pq^4 - q^5$

(c) $(3x + y)^4 = (3x)^4 + 4(3x)^3y + 6(3x)^2y^2 + 4(3x)y^3 + y^4$
$$= 81x^4 + 108x^3y + 54x^2y^2 + 12xy^3 + y^4$$

(d) $(1 + z)^6 = 1 + 6z + 15z^2 + 20z^3 + 15z^4 + 6z^5 + z^6$

2 (a) $(a + b)^3 = a^3 + 3a^2b + 3ab^2 + b^3$
$(a - b)^3 = a^3 - 3a^2b + 3ab^2 - b^3$

(b) Adding the results in part (a),
$$(a + b)^3 + (a - b)^3 = 2a^3 + 6ab^2 = 2a(a^2 + 3b^2)$$

(c) Subtracting the results in part (a),
$$(a + b)^3 - (a - b)^3 = 6a^2b + 2b^3 = 2b(3a^2 + b^2)$$

3E (a) $p = a + b$ and $q = a - b$
$\Rightarrow a = \frac{1}{2}(p + q)$ and $b = \frac{1}{2}(p - q)$
Then $p^3 + q^3 = 2[\frac{1}{2}(p + q)][(\frac{1}{2}(p + q))^2 + 3(\frac{1}{2}(p - q))^2]$
$$= (p + q)(p^2 - pq + q^2)$$

(b) $p^3 - q^3 = (p + (-q))(p^2 - p(-q) + (-q)^2)$
$$= (p - q)(p^2 + pq + q^2)$$

4E Writing 11 as 10 + 1,
$11^2 = (10 + 1)^2 = 10^2 + 2 \times 10 + 1 = 121$
$11^3 = (10 + 1)^3 = 10^3 + 3 \times 10^2 \times 1 + 3 \times 10 \times 1^2 + 1^3 = 1331$
$11^4 = (10 + 1)^4 = 10^4 + 4 \times 10^3 \times 1 + 6 \times 10^2 \times 1^2 + 4 \times 10 \times 1^3 + 1^4$
$$= 14641$$

3.2 Binomial coefficients

EXERCISE 2

1 (a) $\dbinom{8}{3} = \dfrac{8!}{3!\,5!} = \dfrac{8 \times 7 \times 6 \times 5!}{3 \times 2 \times 1 \times 5!} = 56$

(b) $\dbinom{5}{2} = 10$

(c) $\dbinom{9}{6} = \dbinom{9}{3} = 84$

(d) $\dbinom{100}{98} = \dbinom{100}{2} = \dfrac{100 \times 99}{2} = 4950$

2 $(a + b)^7 = a^7 + 7a^6b + 21a^5b^2 + 35a^4b^3 + 35a^3b^4 + 21a^2b^5 + 7ab^6 + b^7$

3 (a) $(a - b)^8 = a^8 - 8a^7b + 28a^6b^2 - 56a^5b^3 + \ldots$

(b) $(2a - 3b)^{10} = (2a)^{10} - 10(2a)^9(3b) + 45(2a)^8(3b)^2 - 120(2a)^7(3b)^3 + \ldots$
$$= 1024a^{10} - 15\,360a^9b + 103\,680a^8b^2 - 414\,720\,a^7b^3 + \ldots$$

(c) $\left(x^2 - \dfrac{1}{x^2}\right)^6 = (x^2)^6 - 6(x^2)^5 \left(\dfrac{1}{x^2}\right) + 15(x^2)^4 \left(\dfrac{1}{x^2}\right)^2 - 20(x^2)^3 \left(\dfrac{1}{x^2}\right)^3 + \ldots$
$$= x^{12} - 6x^8 + 15x^4 - 20 + \ldots$$

4 $a = 11$ from the symmetry of the binomial coefficients.

5 (a) $\dfrac{100!}{80!} \times \dfrac{78!}{99!} = \dfrac{100!}{99!} \times \dfrac{78!}{80!} = \dfrac{100}{1} \times \dfrac{1}{80 \times 79} = 0.0158$

(b) $\dbinom{80}{20} \div \dbinom{80}{19} = \left(\dfrac{80!}{20!\,60!}\right) \div \left(\dfrac{80!}{19!\,61!}\right) = \dfrac{19!\,61!}{20!\,60!} = \dfrac{61}{20} = 3.05$

6E (a) $\dbinom{9}{3} = 84,$ $\dbinom{9}{4} = 126,$ $\dbinom{10}{4} = 210 = \dbinom{9}{3} + \dbinom{9}{4}$

(b) $\dbinom{n+1}{r} = \dbinom{n}{r} + \dbinom{n}{r-1}$

$\dbinom{n}{r} = \dfrac{n!}{(n-r)!\,r!} = \dfrac{n!\,(n-r+1)}{(n-r+1)!r!}$

and $\dbinom{n}{r-1} = \dfrac{n!}{(n-r+1)!\,(r-1)!} = \dfrac{n!\,r}{(n-r+1)!\,r!}$

So $\dbinom{n}{r} + \dbinom{n}{r-1} = \dfrac{n!\,(n-r+1) + n!\,r}{(n-r+1)!\,r!}$

$$= \dfrac{(n+1)!}{(n+1-r)!\,r!}$$

$$= \dbinom{n+1}{r}$$

3.3   Binomial series

> For what range of x is the expansion valid?

$-1 < -2x < 1$
$\Rightarrow -\frac{1}{2} < -x < \frac{1}{2}$
$\Rightarrow -\frac{1}{2} < x < \frac{1}{2}$

You could try plotting $y = \sqrt[3]{(1 - 2x)}$ and $y = 1 - \dfrac{2}{3}x - \dfrac{4}{9}x^2 - \dfrac{40}{81}x^3$

on the same axes to see the range of x for which the first four terms of the expansion give a good approximation to $\sqrt[3]{(1 - 2x)}$.

EXERCISE 3

1   (a) $(1 + x)^{\frac{1}{3}} = 1 + \dfrac{1}{3}x + \dfrac{(\frac{1}{3})(-\frac{2}{3})}{2!}x^2 + \dfrac{(\frac{1}{3})(-\frac{2}{3})(-\frac{5}{3})}{3!}x^3 + \ldots$

$= 1 + \dfrac{1}{3}x - \dfrac{1}{9}x^2 + \dfrac{5}{81}x^3 \ldots$

(b) $(1 + x)^{-3} = 1 + (-3)x + \dfrac{(-3)(-4)}{2!}x^2 + \dfrac{(-3)(-4)(-5)}{3!}x^3 + \ldots$

$= 1 - 3x + 6x^2 - 10x^3 + \ldots$

2   (a) $(1 + x)^{\frac{1}{2}}$ (b) $(1 + x)^{-3}$ (c) $(1 + x)^{\frac{1}{5}}$ (d) $(1 + x)^{-\frac{1}{3}}$

3   (a) $1 - 4x + 10x^2 - 20x^3$

(b) $1 - x - \dfrac{1}{2}x^2 - \dfrac{1}{2}x^3$

(c) $1 - \dfrac{1}{2}x^2$

4   (a) $\sqrt{(9 - 18x)} = \sqrt{(9(1 - 2x))} = \sqrt{9}\,\sqrt{(1 - 2x)} = 3\sqrt{(1 - 2x)}$

(b) $\sqrt{(9 - 18x)} = 3(1 - 2x)^{\frac{1}{2}} = 3(1 + \dfrac{1}{2}(-2x) + \dfrac{(\frac{1}{2})(-\frac{1}{2})}{2!}(-2x)^2 +$

$\dfrac{(\frac{1}{2})(-\frac{1}{2})(-\frac{3}{2})}{3!}(-2x)^3 + \ldots)$

$= 3 - 3x - \dfrac{3}{2}x^2 - \dfrac{3}{2}x^3 \ldots$

$-1 < 2x < 1 \Rightarrow -\dfrac{1}{2} < x < \dfrac{1}{2}$

5   (a) $\dfrac{1}{2}(1 + x)^{-\frac{1}{2}} = \dfrac{1}{2} - \dfrac{1}{4}x + \dfrac{3}{16}x^2$

(b) $\dfrac{1}{9}(1 + x)^{-2} = \dfrac{1}{9} - \dfrac{2}{9}x + \dfrac{1}{3}x^2$

6   (a) The binomial series is only valid for $-1 < x < 1$.

(b) $7\sqrt{\left(1 + \dfrac{1}{49}\right)} = \sqrt{\left(49\left(1 + \dfrac{1}{49}\right)\right)} = \sqrt{50}$

$\sqrt{50} = 7\left(1 + \dfrac{1}{2}\left(\dfrac{1}{49}\right) - \dfrac{1}{8}\left(\dfrac{1}{49}\right)^2 + \dfrac{1}{16}\left(\dfrac{1}{49}\right)^3 \ldots\right) \approx 7.071068$

7E (a) $(1+x)^{\frac{1}{2}} \approx 1 + \frac{1}{2}x \Rightarrow \left(1 - \frac{v^2}{c^2}\right)^{\frac{1}{2}} \approx 1 + \frac{1}{2}\left(-\frac{v^2}{c^2}\right) = 1 - \frac{v^2}{2c^2}$

(b) $\frac{7}{8} = 1 - \frac{v^2}{2c^2} \Rightarrow \frac{v^2}{2c^2} = \frac{1}{8} \Rightarrow v = \frac{1}{2}c$

3.4 Error and relative error

EXERCISE 4

1 (a) $\quad 2a \quad = (20 \pm 0.4) - (19 \pm 0.2)$
$\qquad\qquad = 1 \pm 0.6$
$\Rightarrow a \quad = 0.5 \pm 0.3$
$\Rightarrow \text{area} = (0.5 \pm 0.3)(19 \pm 0.2)$
$\qquad\qquad = 0.5(1 \pm 0.6) \times 19(1 \pm 0.01)$
$\qquad\qquad \approx 9.5(1 \pm 0.61)$
$\qquad\qquad \approx 9.5 \pm 5.8$

(b) The calculation is inaccurate because the relative error of a is large.

2 $\quad h = (125 \pm 2.5) \div \dfrac{(17 \pm 0.5 + 8 \pm 0.5)}{2}$

$\qquad = (125 \pm 2.5) \div \dfrac{(25 \pm 1)}{2}$

$\qquad = 125\,(1 \pm 0.02) \div 12.5\,(1 \pm 0.04)$
$\qquad \approx 10\,(1 \pm 0.06)$
$\qquad \approx 10 \pm 0.6\,\text{cm}$

3 $\quad \text{Speed} = \dfrac{50 \pm 0.5}{1.32 \pm 0.1} \approx \dfrac{50\,(1 \pm 0.01)}{1.32\,(1 \pm 0.076)}$

$\qquad\qquad\qquad \approx 37.9\,(1 \pm 0.086)$
$\qquad\qquad\qquad \approx 37.9 \pm 3.3\,\text{cm\,s}^{-1}$

4 The chain rule

4.1 Functions of functions

For a spherical balloon of radius r cm, the volume in cm^3 is given by

$$V = \frac{4}{3}\pi r^3$$

If the balloon is filled with air at the rate of 200 cm^3 per second, what will be the volume t seconds after inflation is started?

Combine these two equations to obtain a relationship between r and t. Sketch the graph of (t, r). Did you make the correct choice in the section above?

Sketch graphs of (r, V) and (t, V).

Can you think of a way to represent all three relationships in one diagram?

The volume after t seconds is $200t$.

So $200t = \dfrac{4}{3}\pi r^3$

$\Rightarrow r = \sqrt[3]{\left(\dfrac{150t}{\pi}\right)}$

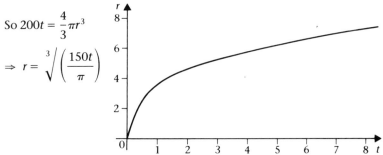

The middle graph on the page was the correct choice.

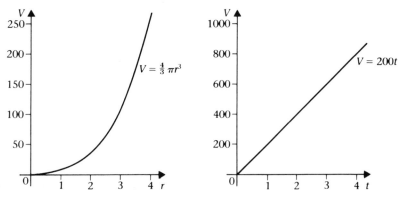

For a single diagram, you could use a three-dimensional curve with respect to axes t, r and V.

EXERCISE 1

1 (a) $y = (x - 2)^2$ (b) $y = 3 \sin x$ (c) $y = e^{2x}$

2 (a) $x \longrightarrow$ | square | $\longrightarrow$ | $\times 2$ | $\longrightarrow y$

(b) $x \longrightarrow$ | $\times 3$ | $\longrightarrow$ | exponential | $\longrightarrow y$

(c) $x \longrightarrow$ | sine | $\longrightarrow$ | square | $\longrightarrow y$

3 (a) $(2x)^2 = 4x^2$ (b) $\sin^2 x$

(c) $\sin(x^2)$ (d) $\sin 2x$

4 (a) $f(x) = 3x$ $g(x) = x^2$

(b) $f(x) = \tan x$ $g(x) = 3x$

(c) $f(x) = x^2$ $g(x) = \cos x$

(d) $f(x) = e^x$ $g(x) = x^2$

4.2 Chain rule

> You have seen that the chain rule holds for linear functions.
> Why might you expect it to hold more generally?

If you zoom in at any chosen point on a locally straight function, then it will look increasingly like a linear function. You might, therefore, expect the chain rule to be true for any **locally straight** functions.

EXERCISE 2

1 (a) $\dfrac{dR}{dt} = 2t$ $\dfrac{dS}{dR} = 2R$

$\dfrac{dS}{dt} = 4Rt = 4t(3 + t^2)$

(b) $S = 9 + 6t^2 + t^4$

$\dfrac{dS}{dt} = 12t + 4t^3$

$= 4t(3 + t^2)$

2 By the chain rule: let $R = 5 + 4t \Rightarrow S = R^3$

$\dfrac{dR}{dt} = 4$ $\dfrac{dS}{dR} = 3R^2$

$\dfrac{dS}{dt} = 12R^2$

$= 12(5 + 4t)^2$

By expanding:
$$S = (25 + 40t + 16t^2)(5 + 4t)$$
$$= 125 + 300t + 240t^2 + 64t^3$$
$$\Rightarrow \quad \frac{dS}{dt} = 300 + 480t + 192t^2$$
$$= 12(25 + 40t + 16t^2)$$
$$= 12(5 + 4t)^2$$

The chain rule is preferable!

3 Let $R = 4 + 3t^2 \Rightarrow \dfrac{dR}{dt} = 6t$

$\qquad S = R^3 \qquad \Rightarrow \dfrac{dS}{dR} = 3R^2$

$\qquad\qquad\qquad\qquad \dfrac{dS}{dt} = 18t(4 + 3t^2)^2$

4 $\dfrac{dy}{du} = \cos u, \qquad \dfrac{du}{dx} = 2$

$\quad \dfrac{dy}{dx} = 2 \cos u$

$\qquad\quad = 2 \cos 2x$

5 Let $u = 3x, \qquad y = \cos u$

$\quad \dfrac{dy}{dx} = 3 \times -\sin u$

$\qquad\quad = -3 \sin 3x$

6 Let $u = ax, \qquad y = \sin u$

$\quad \dfrac{dy}{dx} = a \cos u$

$\qquad\quad = a \cos ax$

7 (a) Let $u = 3x, \qquad y = e^u$

$\qquad \dfrac{dy}{dx} = 3e^u$

$\qquad\qquad = 3e^{3x}$

$\quad$ (b) Let $u = \sin x, \qquad y = u^2$

$\qquad \dfrac{dy}{dx} = \cos x \times 2u$

$\qquad\qquad = 2 \sin x \cos x$

8 (a) $2xe^{x^2}$ $\quad$ (b) $-6 \sin 2x$ $\quad$ (c) $12x(x^2 + 1)^2$

9 (a) $\dfrac{dV}{dt} = 200 \qquad \dfrac{dV}{dr} = 4\pi r^2$

(b) $200 = 4\pi r^2 \dfrac{dr}{dt}$

$\dfrac{dr}{dt} = \dfrac{50}{\pi r^2}$

When $t = 1$, $V = 200$

$\Rightarrow 200 = \dfrac{4}{3}\pi r^3$

$\Rightarrow r = 3.63$

$\Rightarrow \dfrac{dr}{dt} = \dfrac{50}{\pi \times 3.63^2}$

$\qquad\qquad = 1.21\,\text{cm s}^{-1}$ (to 2 decimal places)

10 (a) $r = 3 + 0.04t^2$ ① $\Rightarrow \dfrac{dr}{dt} = 0.08t$

Assuming the balloon is spherical,

$V = \dfrac{4}{3}\pi r^3 \Rightarrow \dfrac{dV}{dr} = 4\pi r^2$

(b) $\dfrac{dV}{dt} = \dfrac{dV}{dr} \times \dfrac{dr}{dt}$

$\dfrac{dV}{dt} = 4\pi r^2 \times 0.08t$

(c) When $t = 2$, $r = 3.16$ from ①

$\Rightarrow \dfrac{dV}{dt} = 0.32\pi \times (3.16)^2 \times 2$

$\dfrac{dV}{dt} = 20.1\,\text{m}^3$ per minute   (to 3 s.f.)

11 (a) $V = x^3$

$\dfrac{dV}{dx} = 3x^2$

(b) $\dfrac{dx}{dt} = -0.5,$ $\dfrac{dV}{dt} = -1.5x^2$

$\qquad\qquad\qquad\qquad \dfrac{dV}{dt} = -1.5(4 - 0.5t)^2$

(c) When $t = 2$, $\dfrac{dV}{dt} = -13.5\,\text{cm}^3$ per hour

4.3 Differentiation by inspection

EXERCISE 3

1 (a) $\dfrac{dy}{dx} = 4(2x)(x^2 + 3)^3$

$\qquad\qquad = 8x(x^2 + 3)^3$

(b) $\dfrac{dy}{dx} = 5 \times 2(5 + 2x)^4$

$\qquad = 10(5 + 2x)^4$

(c) $\dfrac{dy}{dx} = 3(4x - 3)(2x^2 - 3x)^2$

(d) $\dfrac{dy}{dx} = 4(3x^2 - 6x)(x^3 - 3x^2)^3$

$\qquad = 12x^7(x - 2)(x - 3)^3$

2 (a) $-2x \sin x^2; \ 0$ (b) $2 \cos 2x; \ 2$ (c) $3e^{3x}; \ 3$

3 (a) $-3x^2 \sin x^3$ (b) $3 \sin^2 x \cos x$ (c) $-8 \cos^3 x \sin x$

4E (a) $2 \times 2 \sin 2x \times \cos 2x = 4 \sin 2x \cos 2x$

     (b) $3 \times 4 \times 2 \cos 4x \times (-\sin 4x) = -24 \cos 4x \sin 4x$

     (c) $\cos x \times e^{\sin x}$

4.4 Applications to integration

E X E R C I S E   4

1 (a) $\dfrac{1}{3} \sin 3x + c$

This is an indefinite integral and so the constant of integration must be included.

(b) $-2 \cos \dfrac{1}{2} x + c$ (c) $-\dfrac{2}{5} \cos 5x + c$ (d) $\dfrac{1}{2} e^{2x} + c$

2 (a) $\left[2e^{0.5x} \right]_1^2 = (2e) - (2e^{0.5}) = 2.14$ (to 2 decimal places)

(b) $\left[-\dfrac{1}{2} \cos 2x \right]_{-1}^0 = \left(-\dfrac{1}{2} \right) - \left(-\dfrac{1}{2} \cos (-2) \right) = -0.71$ (to 2 decimal places)

Note: the angle is in radians

(c) $\left[6 \sin \dfrac{x}{2} \right]_0^2 = (6 \sin 1) - (0) = 5.05$ (to 2 decimal places)

(d) $\left[\dfrac{1}{6} (2x + 3)^3 \right]_0^1 = \left(\dfrac{1}{6} \times 125 \right) - \left(\dfrac{1}{6} \times 27 \right) = \dfrac{98}{6} = 16\dfrac{1}{3}$

3 (a) A is $\left(\dfrac{\pi}{2}, 0 \right)$, $\displaystyle\int_0^{\pi/2} \sin 2x \, dx = \left[-0.5 \cos 2x \right]_0^{\pi/2} = 1$

(b) B is $(\pi, 0)$, $\displaystyle\int_0^\pi \frac{1}{2}\cos\frac{1}{2}x\,dx = \left[\sin\frac{1}{2}x\right]_0^\pi = 1$

(c) C is $\left(\dfrac{\pi}{4}, 0\right)$, $\displaystyle\int_0^{\pi/4} 3\sin 2x\,dx = \left[-1.5\cos 2x\right]_0^{\pi/4} = 1.5$

4E   The result is **not** true.

$\displaystyle\int_1^2 \cos x^2\,dx = -0.44$ (to 2 decimal places) by the trapezium rule

and $\left[\dfrac{1}{2x}\sin x^2\right]_1^2 = -0.61$ (to 2 decimal places)

$\dfrac{d}{dx}\left(\dfrac{1}{2x}\sin x^2\right) \neq \cos x^2$

5E   (a) $2\sin\dfrac{1}{2}x + c$ (b) $\dfrac{2}{5}e^{2.5x} + c$

(c) Not possible by the methods of this chapter. The expression would have to be multiplied out before it could be integrated.

(d) $\dfrac{1}{25}(5x+3)^5 + c$ (e) $-\dfrac{1}{5}\cos 5x + c$ (f) not possible

6E   (a) $-\dfrac{1}{2}\cos x^2 + c$ (b) $\dfrac{1}{3}e^{x^3} + c$

(c) $\dfrac{1}{10}(2x^2+1)^5 + c$

7E $= \displaystyle\int_0^1 \frac{1}{2}(1 - \cos 2x)\,dx$

$= \left[\dfrac{x}{2} - \dfrac{1}{4}\sin 2x\right]_0^1$

$= \left(\dfrac{1}{2} - \dfrac{1}{4}\sin 2\right) - (0)$

$= 0.27$ (to 2 decimal places)

4.5   Inverse functions and x^n

> (a) Show the derivative of $\dfrac{1}{x^2}$ is $-\dfrac{2}{x^3}$.
>
> (b) Find the derivative of $\sqrt{x}(1 + x)$.

(a) $y = \dfrac{1}{x^2} = x^{-2} \Rightarrow \dfrac{dy}{dx} = -2x^{-3} = -\dfrac{2}{x^3}$

(b) An expression such as $\sqrt{x}(1 + x)$ must be multiplied out before it can be differentiated.

$y = \sqrt{x}(1 + x) = \sqrt{x} + \sqrt{x}\,x = x^{\frac{1}{2}} + x^{\frac{3}{2}}$

Then $\dfrac{dy}{dx} = \dfrac{1}{2}x^{-\frac{1}{2}} + \dfrac{3}{2}x^{\frac{1}{2}} = \dfrac{1}{2\sqrt{x}} + \dfrac{3}{2}\sqrt{x}$

EXERCISE 5

1 (a) $\dfrac{1}{3}x^{-\frac{2}{3}}$ (b) $-x^{-2}$ (c) $-3x^{-4}$ (d) $-2x^{-3} + \dfrac{1}{2}x^{-\frac{1}{2}}$

2 $y = x^{\frac{1}{n}} \Rightarrow \dfrac{dy}{dx} = \dfrac{1}{n}x^{\frac{1}{n} - 1}$

3 Let $u = 2x \quad \Rightarrow \quad \dfrac{du}{dx} = 2$

$y = \ln u \Rightarrow \dfrac{dy}{du} = \dfrac{1}{u}$

$\dfrac{dy}{dx} = \dfrac{\cancel{2}}{\cancel{2}x} = \dfrac{1}{x}$

4 (a) $y = \ln 3x \Rightarrow \dfrac{dy}{dx} = \dfrac{1}{x}$

$y = \ln 5x \Rightarrow \dfrac{dy}{dx} = \dfrac{1}{x}$

(b) $y = \ln ax \Rightarrow \dfrac{dy}{dx} = \dfrac{1}{x}$

(c) $\qquad y = \ln ax$

$\Rightarrow \quad y = \ln a + \ln x \qquad$ [because $\ln (A \times B) = \ln A + \ln B$]

$\Rightarrow \dfrac{dy}{dx} = 0 + \dfrac{1}{x} \qquad$ [$\ln a$ is a constant value and so has a zero derivative]

5 (a) $\int \dfrac{1}{2x}\,dx = \dfrac{1}{2}\ln x + c$ (b) $\dfrac{1}{a}\ln x + c$

6E $\dfrac{dx}{dy} = e^y = x$

Then $\dfrac{dy}{dx} = \dfrac{1}{dx/dy} = \dfrac{1}{x}$

7E $\dfrac{dx}{dy} = 3y^2$

$\dfrac{dy}{dx} = \dfrac{1}{3y^2}$

$\dfrac{dy}{dx} = \dfrac{1}{3(\sqrt[3]{x})^2} = \dfrac{1}{3}x^{-\frac{2}{3}}$

8E (a) $\dfrac{dx}{dy} = \cos y \;\Rightarrow\; \dfrac{dy}{dx} = \dfrac{1}{\cos y}$

(b) The third side is $\sqrt{(1 - x^2)}$.

Therefore $\cos y = \sqrt{(1 - x^2)}$ and $\dfrac{dy}{dx} = \dfrac{1}{\sqrt{(1 - x^2)}}$.

(c) For $y = \cos^{-1}x$, $\dfrac{dy}{dx} = \dfrac{-1}{\sqrt{(1 - x^2)}}$

9E $r = \left(\dfrac{150t}{\pi}\right)^{\frac{1}{3}}$ $t = \dfrac{\pi r^3}{150}$

$\dfrac{dr}{dt} = \left(\dfrac{150t}{\pi}\right)^{-\frac{2}{3}} \times \dfrac{150}{\pi}$ $\dfrac{dt}{dr} = \dfrac{3\pi r^2}{150}$

$\dfrac{dr}{dt} = \dfrac{1}{3}(r^3)^{-\frac{2}{3}} \times \dfrac{150}{\pi}$ $\dfrac{dr}{dt} = \dfrac{50}{\pi r^2}$

This agrees with the earlier answer which was found in terms of r.

5 Differential equations

5.1 Introduction

Explain the meaning of each of the symbols used in the formulation of the law given above.

y is the difference in temperature between the object and its surroundings.

$\dfrac{dy}{dt}$ is the rate of change of the difference in temperature between the object and its surroundings, with respect to time.

$-k$ is the constant of proportionality. This is negative since the object is cooling.

EXERCISE 1

1

x	-3	-2	-1	0	1	2	3
$\dfrac{dy}{dx}$	-1.5	-1.0	-0.5	0	0.5	1.0	1.5

(a) $\dfrac{dy}{dx} = 0.5x$

(c) $y = 0.25x^2 + 1.5$, $\quad y = 0.25x^2$, $\quad y = 0.25x^2 - 4$

$\dfrac{dy}{dx} = 0.5x$ for each of the curves.

2 (a) $\dfrac{dy}{dx} = 0.5y$

(b)

x	-3	-2	-1	0
y	0.2	0.4	0.6	1
$\dfrac{dy}{dx}$	0.1	0.2	0.3	0.5

All the gradients agree with the formula.

(c) At $y = 3$, all the gradients should be 1.5.

5.2 Algebraic solutions

EXERCISE 2

1 (a) $y = e^x + c$

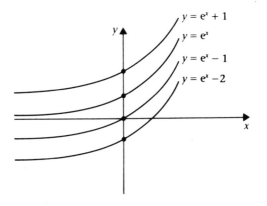

151

(b) $y = \dfrac{1}{2}\sin 2x + c$

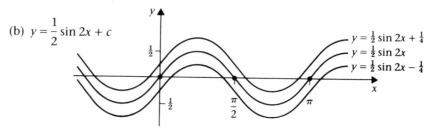

$y = \frac{1}{2}\sin 2x + \frac{1}{4}$
$y = \frac{1}{2}\sin 2x$
$y = \frac{1}{2}\sin 2x - \frac{1}{4}$

(c) $\dfrac{dy}{dx} = \dfrac{-1}{x^2} \Rightarrow y = \dfrac{1}{x} + c$

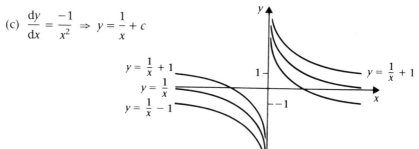

$y = \frac{1}{x} + 1$
$y = \frac{1}{x}$
$y = \frac{1}{x} - 1$

$y = \frac{1}{x} + 1$

2 (a) $y = x^4 - 1$ when $x = 3, y = 80$

(b) $y = x^3 - x^2 + 2x - 2$ when $x = 3, y = 22$

(c) $y = \dfrac{1}{2} - \dfrac{1}{2}x^{-2}$ when $x = 3, y = \dfrac{4}{9}$

(d) $y = e^{2x} - e^2$ when $x = 3, y \approx 396$

3 (a) $y = 8t - \dfrac{2t^2}{3} + 32$ so when $t = 4, y = 53\dfrac{1}{3}$

(b) $\dfrac{dy}{dt} = 0$ when $t = 6$. After this time, $\dfrac{dy}{dt} < 0$ and so the water is no longer being heated. The model is probably no longer valid.

4E (a) $y = -\dfrac{1}{3}\cos(3x + 2) - 0.139$ (to 3 d.p.)   when $x = 2, y \approx -0.090$

(b) $y = \dfrac{1}{3}e^{x^3} - \dfrac{1}{3}$ when $x = 2, y \approx 993$

(c) $y = \dfrac{1}{2}\sin(x^2 + 1) - 0.421$ (to 3 d.p.)   when $x = 2, y \approx -0.900$

5.3 Direction diagrams

EXERCISE 3

1 The curves are a family of ellipses.

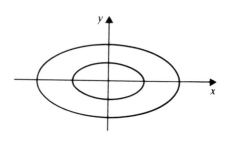

2 The curves are similar to that of the Normal distribution in statistics.

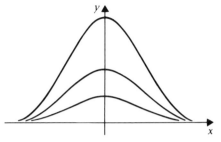

3 x represents the mass of reacting substance at time t.

$\dfrac{dx}{dt}$ represents the rate at which the mass is changing, i.e. the rate of reaction.

$\dfrac{dx}{dt} = -kx$ represents the fact that the rate of loss of mass is proportional to the mass.

$\dfrac{dx}{dt} = -0.5x$

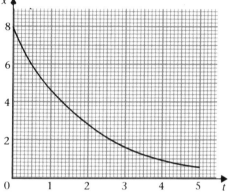

8 is the value of x at time $t = 0$, i.e. the initial mass of the substance.

5.4 Numerical methods

> What is the gradient at (1.1, 4.2)?
>
> Find the step up for a further step along of $dx = 0.1$. What point along the tangent at (1.1, 4.2) is now reached?

The gradient at (1.1, 4.2) is $2 \times 1.1 = 2.2$.
The step up is $2.2 \times 0.1 = 0.22$.
The point along the tangent at (1.1, 4.2) that is now reached is (1.2, 4.42).

> When $x = 1.5$, what value of y is found by moving along tangents with steps of $dx = 0.1$?
>
> What is the value for y on the actual solution curve through (1, 4)? How could the accuracy of the step-by-step method have been improved, if necessary?

153

The table of values is:

	x	y	$\dfrac{dy}{dx}$	dx	dy	$x + dx$	$y + dy$
First step	1	4	2	0.1	0.2	1.1	4.2
Second step	1.1	4.2	2.2	0.1	0.22	1.2	4.42
Third step	1.2	4.42	2.4	0.1	0.24	1.3	4.66
Fourth step	1.3	4.66	2.6	0.1	0.26	1.4	4.92
Fifth step	1.4	4.92	2.8	0.1	0.28	1.5	5.20
Sixth step	1.5	5.20					

When $x = 1.5$, $y = 5.20$
The actual solution curve is $y = x^2 + 3$.
When $x = 1.5$, $y = 2.25 + 3 = 5.25$
Taking smaller steps, such as $dx = 0.05$ or $dx = 0.01$, will improve the accuracy.

Continue the calculations to obtain $y = 7.64$ when $x = 2$.

x	y	$\dfrac{dy}{dx}$	dx	dy	$x + dx$	$y + dy$
1	6	3	0.2	0.6	1.2	6.6
1.2	6.6	2.15	0.2	0.43	1.4	7.03
1.4	7.03	1.45	0.2	0.29	1.6	7.32
1.6	7.32	0.97	0.2	0.19	1.8	7.51
1.8	7.51	0.65	0.2	0.13	2.0	7.64
2.0	7.64					

EXERCISE 4

1 (a) $y = \sin x$

(b)

x	0	0.5	1.0	1.5	2.0	2.5	3.0	3.5	4.0	4.5	5.0
Numerical y	0	0.5	0.9	1.0	1.0	0.7	0.2	−0.3	−0.7	−0.9	−0.9
Exact y	0	0.5	0.8	1.0	0.9	0.6	0.1	−0.4	−0.8	−1.0	−1.0

From the table you can see that the numerical and exact values appear to differ by at most 0.1.

2 (a) $y = x^4 + c \Rightarrow y = x^4 - 1$
When $x = 2$, $y = 15$.

(b) To 1 decimal place, successive points are
$(1, 0)$, $(1.2, 0.8)$, $(1.4, 2.2)$, $(1.6, 4.4)$, $(1.8, 7.7)$, $(2, 12.3)$
When $x = 2$, $y \approx 12.3$.

3 (a) $y = -\frac{1}{2}\cos 2x$

(b) An exact solution is $-\frac{1}{2}\cos 2 \approx 0.208$
The numerical solution is 0.160.
The percentage error is $\dfrac{0.048}{0.208} \times 100 \approx 23\%$

4 (a) $y = x^2 + 1$

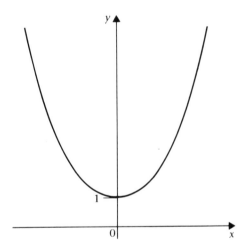

(b) With a step of $dx = 0.2$:

x	1	1.2	1.4	1.6	1.8	2.0	2.2	2.4	2.6	2.8	3.0
y	2	2.4	2.9	3.4	4.1	4.8	5.6	6.5	7.4	8.5	9.6

With a step of $dx = -0.2$:

x	1	0.8	0.6	0.4	0.2	0.0	−0.2	−0.4	−0.6	−0.8	−1.0
y	2	1.6	1.3	1.0	0.9	0.8	0.8	0.9	1.0	1.3	1.6

155

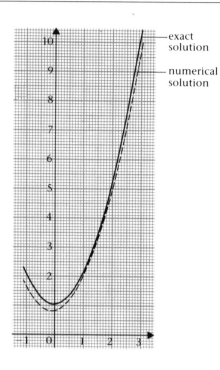

exact
solution

numerical
solution

The numerical solution slightly
underestimates the exact solution.
The error increases as you move away
from (1, 2).

(c) With a step size of 0.1, the numerical solution still underestimates the
    exact solution. However, the smaller step size reduces the error by about
    50%.

5E $dx = 0.2$

x	0	0.2	0.4	0.6	0.8	1.0	1.2	1.4	1.6	1.8	2.0
Numerical y	1	1.2	1.4	1.7	2.1	2.6	3.1	3.8	4.6	5.6	6.8
Exact y	1	1.2	1.5	1.8	2.2	2.7	3.3	4.1	5.0	6.0	7.4

$dx = 0.1$

x	0	0.5	1.0	1.5	2.0	2.5	3.0	3.5	4.0
Numerical y	1	1.6	2.6	4.3	7.1	11.6	19.1	31.5	52.0
Exact y	1	1.6	2.7	4.5	7.4	12.2	20.1	33.1	54.6

6E

x	0	0.5	1.0	1.5	2.0	2.5	3.0	3.5	4.0
y	0	0.5	0.8	1.0	1.1	1.2	1.3	1.3	1.4

x	0	−0.5	−1.0	−1.5	−2.0	−2.5	−3.0	−3.5	−4.0
y	0	−0.5	−0.8	−1.0	−1.1	−1.2	−1.3	−1.3	−1.4

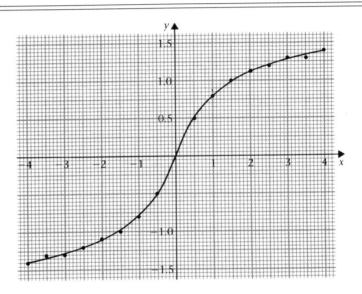

The shape of the 'turned round' graph suggests the tangent function.

The relationship is $y = \tan^{-1}x$.

5.5 Growth and decay

(a) Use the fact that death occurred when $y = 22$ to show that the doctor's estimate of the time of death would be 4:54 a.m.

(b) Compare this answer with that obtained earlier using numerical methods and comment on the discrepancy.

(a) $y = 22 \Rightarrow \quad 22 = 10e^{-0.713t}$
$\Rightarrow \ln 2.2 = -0.713t$
$\Rightarrow \quad t = 1.106$

1.106 hours is 1 hour 6 minutes. The time of death was 1 hour 6 minutes before 6:00 a.m.

(b) The earlier answer in tasksheet 2 estimated death as taking place 1.3 hours before 6:00 a.m. The main error is not in the numerical step-by-step method, but in estimating λ as −0.6 instead of −0.713.

EXERCISE 5

1 $y = Ae^{-x}$
$y = 2$ when $x = 0$, therefore $A = 2$
$y = 2e^{-x}$

2 (a) $x = Ae^{-0.1t} \Rightarrow x = 2e^{-0.1t}$

(b) $1 = 2e^{-0.1t}$
$\Rightarrow e^{-0.1t} = 0.5$
$\Rightarrow -0.1t = \ln 0.5$
$\Rightarrow -0.1t \approx -0.693$
$\Rightarrow \quad t \approx 6.93$ hours
It takes approximately 6 hours 56 minutes.

3 Assume Newton's laws of cooling.
y is the temperature in °C above room temperature,
t is the time in minutes after boiling.

$$\frac{dy}{dt} = \lambda y \Rightarrow y = Ae^{\lambda t}$$

$t = 0 \quad y = 80 \Rightarrow A = 80$

$t = 5 \quad y = 70 \Rightarrow 70 = 80e^{5\lambda}$

$$\Rightarrow \lambda = \frac{1}{5} \ln \left(\frac{70}{80} \right) = -0.0267$$

The water cools to 60°C when $y = 40$.
$40 = 80e^{-0.0267t} \Rightarrow t = 26$ minutes

4 The differential equation is $\dfrac{dN}{dt} = \lambda N$
N is the number of insects,
t is the time in days.

When $N = 100$, $\dfrac{dN}{dt} = 50 \Rightarrow \lambda = 0.5$

$$\frac{dN}{dt} = 0.5N \Rightarrow N = Ae^{0.5t}$$

When $t = 0$, $N = 100 \Rightarrow A = 100$
Therefore $N = 100e^{0.5t}$ and so when $t = 10$, $N = 14841$
There will be nearly 15000 insects after 10 days.

5 (a) $\dfrac{dm}{dt} = \lambda m$ when $m = 0.020$, $\dfrac{dm}{dt} = -0.001 \Rightarrow \lambda = -0.05$

The differential equation is $\dfrac{dm}{dt} = -0.05m$

(b) $\dfrac{dm}{dt} = -0.05m \Rightarrow m = Ae^{-0.05t}$

A is the mass when $t = 0$, so $A = 0.020 \Rightarrow m = 0.020e^{-0.05t}$
When $m = 0.010$, $\quad 0.010 = 0.020e^{-0.05t}$
$$\Rightarrow t = -20\ln 0.5$$
$$= 13.86$$

The substance will decay to half its mass after 13.86 days. This is called the **half-life** of the substance.

5.6 Formulating differential equations

EXERCISE 6

1 (a) For a snowball of radius r cm and time t days

$$\dfrac{dV}{dt} = -4k\pi r^2 \Rightarrow \dfrac{dr}{dt} = -k$$

(b) $r = c - kt$
$r = 30$ when $t = 0$ and $r = 0$ when $t = 10$, so $r = 30 - 3t$

(i) $15 = 30 - 3t \Rightarrow t = 5$
The radius will be halved after 5 days.

(ii) $\dfrac{30}{\sqrt[3]{2}} = 30 - 3t \Rightarrow t = 2.1$
The volume will be halved after 2.1 days.

2 (a) $0.1 = 10\%$ -0.1 is used because there is a reduction of 10%. $\alpha = 2000$.

(b) y is the number of fish and $\dfrac{dy}{dt}$ is the change in the number of fish per year.

(c) About 16 years

(d) $\dfrac{dy}{dt} = 2500 - 0.12y$

3E V is the volume of liquid in the urn in cupfuls.
t is the time in seconds.

The rate of change of volume, $\dfrac{dV}{dt}$, is proportional to the square root of V (assuming that the urn has a constant cross-section).

So $\dfrac{dV}{dt} = -\lambda\sqrt{V}$, where λ is a constant.

Numerical method

When $V = 100$, $\quad \dfrac{dV}{dt} \approx -\dfrac{9}{60}$ cups per second

$\Rightarrow \quad -\dfrac{9}{60} \approx -\lambda \sqrt{100}$

$\Rightarrow \quad \lambda \approx 0.015$

You need the solution curve through $(0, 100)$ and require t when $V = 52$ (when 48 cups have been filled).

With a step of $dt = 1$ (second), this occurs after 6 minutes 12 seconds.

Analytical method

$$\dfrac{dV}{dt} = -\lambda \sqrt{V}$$

$$\Rightarrow \quad \dfrac{dt}{dV} = -\dfrac{1}{\lambda \sqrt{V}}$$

$$\Rightarrow \quad t = -\dfrac{2}{\lambda} \sqrt{V} + c$$

When $t = 0$, $\quad V = 100$ and when $t = 60$, $\quad V = 91$

The simultaneous equations give $\lambda = 0.01535$, $\quad c = 1303$.

$$t \approx 1303 - 130.3 \sqrt{V}$$

When $V = 52$,

$$t \approx 363$$

It takes 6 minutes 3 seconds.